Part One

Bet on the Turtle

(My Long, Slow Journey of Faith)

and

Part Two

Reason to Believe

James Weagley

RIVER BIRCH PRESS

Daphne, Alabama

ISBN 978-1-951561-49-9 (Print)
ISBN 978-1-951561-50-5 (Ebook)
For Worldwide Distribution
Printed in the U.S.A.

River Birch Press
P.O. Box 868, Daphne, AL 36526

Table of Contents

Foreword

This book captures many of the hills and valleys that we experience in our faith journey with God. The written vignettes provide the reader with an opportunity to reflect and meditate on those similar scenarios of life. At times, a person's joy and anger are outward responses to their perception of God's intervention during a season in life. These emotional obstacles, including grief, disappointment, and abandonment, are examined as reasons to blame God and disconnect from our faith. The story of Mr. Weagley's turn away from God resonates with my ethnographic studies of reasons why people stop going to church.

Interestingly, it is through others and their faith in God that one can possibly find a path back to God. The journalistic approach found in the memoirs helps the reader connect the stories through a journey of finding faith in God. The strength of this book is found in the storytelling approach of describing the relational action between God and the writer. The reader is welcomed into the audience as a participant in sharing common stories. Additionally, theological interpretation and terms are not needed to comprehend the meaning of each story.

Mr. Weagley spent his vocational years serving both as an educator of health and wellness and as an athletic trainer. God has used his gifts through the years to restore sick bodies and heal broken bones. Metaphorically speaking, this work is his answering of the call-in ministry to heal and restore broken relationships in the Christian faith. Mr. Weagley is responsible, sincere, and honest as he communicates the brokenness and sins of his negative behavior. It is through his self-observation and observations of others in which brokenness of faith leads to a muddled path of self-destruction. Conversely, this must-read illustrates how the return to one's faith can be attained through the very life experiences which caused the initial conflict in their faith.

I recommend *Bet on the Turtle* as a memoir of study for anyone fighting God when it seems that He has not shown up during their life's battles. This book should not be analyzed on the merits of just biblical hermeneutics. To the contrary, this work demonstrates a methodology of how scripture can be actualized in our faith journey.

— *Reverend Dr. Linwood M. Smith, Jr.*

PART ONE:
BET ON THE TURTLE

Introduction

My childhood can be described with one word—fantastic. I grew up on a farm that had acres and acres of woods, fields, streams, and waterfalls. We explored, hiked, and camped. We swam, ice skated, and went sledding. We had plenty of space to play our childhood games. It was Kid Heaven!

I was blessed to be part of a loving family, consisting of my parents, two older brothers, and younger sister. We also had the loving companionship of many furry friends during our childhood.

We lived just a few miles outside of the quaint little rustic town of Mendham, New Jersey. We were members of the St. Joseph Catholic Church community and attended school there. It was a warm, close-knit community that was ideal for family life. It wasn't hard to imagine Sheriff Andy Taylor of Mayberry directing traffic in the town center.

Our blissful existence came crashing down one summer afternoon as the result of a family tragedy. Sadly, we blamed God for what happened and turned away from our church family and Christianity.

The first part of this book is about my childhood experiences growing up in a loving family and attending Catholic school. I also relive the tragedy and share how that experience affected our family. Finally, I talk about my struggles as I drifted through my teen and young adult years, trying to find my way back to faith.

There have been many obstacles and opportunities for growth on my faith journey. Like a turtle, I withdrew into my shell during some scary times and plodded slowly and carefully along the road to faith. Through God's loving grace I am a little further along on that road now.

It is my sincere hope that by reading my story you will be able to identify with me. I was and am in no way perfect. I have struggled and made my share of mistakes. Although I am optimistic it won't happen as often, I fully expect I will continue to make my share of mistakes.

I really hope that reading this book inspires you to examine your own life and faith and then reach out and see how God welcomes you with open arms to share your life with him.

→1←

HIGHS AND LOWS

The righteous person may have many troubles, but the LORD delivers him from them all (Psalm 34:19).

Panic and shock would best describe my immediate reaction to the most difficult moment in the first fourteen years of my life. Before then, I had not experienced anything but an absolutely wonderful childhood, which is pretty amazing. Up until that time, I was blessed to be surrounded by loving family, relatives, and friends and had a magical childhood without any real trauma.

Like anyone, I have had some bad days. But a Sunday afternoon softball game in mid-July 1969 turned out to be the worst. During the middle of the game, we saw my mom running from our house toward us screaming, "John, John!" repeatedly and crying hysterically.

Everyone ran up to the house, and my mother pointed us toward our basement. Stuart, who worked as my father's assistant, my brothers, and I raced down the steps and found my dad unconscious, laying on the floor next to a couch. Stuart performed CPR on my father, and we called 911. I recall the ambulance streaking down our road and up our driveway as we stood around in tears trying to make some sense of what had just happened. My father was taken to Morristown Memorial Hospital, and we were told later that his heart had stopped several times during the trip.

We all have moments in our lives that we can recall with perfect clarity. Some are wonderful and some are painful. For me, some unforgettably great life moments include my wedding day, the birth of my children and grandchildren, and less monumental occasions like getting a hole in one in golf. Unfortunately, just like those wonderful memories; tragic moments can become embedded in our brains as well. Some fifty years later, I am still able to vividly recreate in my mind the images I described above.

I can remember being at the hospital and visiting my dad in the ICU. He was hooked up to what seemed like an endless and tangled collection of wires and machines and was unconscious. I remember feeling hollow and numb. I wasn't sure what to think, say, or feel. It was all pretty overwhelming and confusing.

We found out that my dad had suffered a ruptured cerebral aneurysm in the frontal lobe of his brain. A cerebral aneurysm is a weak spot in the wall of a blood vessel inside the brain that gets worn out and bulges. Although brain aneurysms sound alarming, most don't cause symptoms or health problems, and a lot of people live a long life without ever realizing they even have one. Unfortunately, my father happened to be one of the rare cases.

My dad was scheduled for surgery the next day to clamp off the damaged artery. We waited for what seemed an eternity for the phone to ring with news. We milled around the house, pacing back and forth in a fog from the kitchen to the dining room. Not much was said. Small talk didn't seem right and discussing the "what ifs" of the surgery was too scary. The phone finally rang, and it was our family physician who was kind enough to observe the surgery and report the result to us. I remember tears streaming down my mom's face as she excitedly proclaimed the surgery was successful and things looked good. We hugged and screamed joyously in relief, thrilled that my father was going to be okay.

My dad was in the hospital for a long time; his recovery was slow, and we visited almost every day. At first, he was unconscious and in intensive care. Slowly but surely, he began to improve. Progress was slow but there was definitely measurable improvement every week. His eyes opened, he started moving his fingers and hands, and began to make sounds. The sounds eventually became words and then sentences.

He had to relearn the most basic activities. Self-care tasks like brushing teeth, shaving, dressing, and toileting had to be relearned. I remember very clearly helping him drink and eat and then assisting him as he relearned how to use a knife, fork, and spoon. I can remember the pride I experienced as I helped care for him during his recovery. After an extensive hospital stay, and weeks and weeks of occupational and physical therapy, Dad finally came home.

We were ecstatic that life would finally return to normal. Bit by bit my dad improved. He eventually regained full autonomy with the activities of daily living and gradually returned to work. Looking back now, I think we probably heard what we wanted to hear from the medical staff which was that he was going to okay. In our minds that meant he would be normal, we would have our old dad back again at home with us, and things would be just like they used to be. In reality, things would never be the same.

Our lives had changed forever. My dad's aneurysm was a very significant event in the life of my entire family. It impacted all of us and helped define and shape my life and faith.

This book describes my rather long, slow journey to becoming a Christian. As you will see, the emotional trauma and adjustments for me and my family following my dad's brain aneurysm were dramatic and required a significant adjustment for all of us. It also played a significant role in my relationship with God.

As I look back, I realize that God has been quite patient with me. I have always tended to be a bit critical and cynical and needed proof in order to believe something. I tend to overthink things. Sometimes, my head gets in my way! I am sure that is why it took me so long to become a Christian.

Becoming a Christian has been a very lengthy process with numerous roadblocks and detours. In hindsight I fought a lot along the way. I often took two steps forward and one step back; at times I have taken one step forward and two steps back. I have been very much like the turtle in the Aesop Fable, "The Turtle and the Hare." I have even had times where I stopped and hid in my shell. It has been a slow journey.

I think I have been very similar to Billy, the little boy who is the main character in the Family Circus comic. Billy very much has his own agenda. For example, if his mom asks him to do something, the comic will show him following a rather long, convoluted path where he might ride his bike, throw a ball for the dog, and do a thousand other things he enjoys doing before he eventually gets there. That has been me, and if this sounds like you, don't worry. I finally found my faith and so can you.

I am hoping that if you are a non-Christian, my story might help you to at the very least begin to think about God. If you are a Christian, I am hoping what you read will affirm and strengthen your faith. I have reached a point in my life where I am confident of the proof of God's existence and much more. This is my story of I how I got there.

➔2🙰

CHILDHOOD MEMORIES

Truly I tell you, unless you change and become like little children, you will never enter the kingdom of Heaven (Matthew 18: 2-6).

As I said, I really had a fantastic childhood. I would describe it as magical. I was blessed to grow up in the wilds of northern New Jersey in a loving home with my parents, John and Marion, two older brothers John and Jeff, and my younger sister, Joanne. Yes, I did say "the wilds of northern New Jersey," and yes there were and still are very nice, rural areas in New Jersey.

Poor New Jersey sometimes suffers from an undeserved inferiority complex. It really is the Rodney Dangerfield of states, getting "no respect." For those whose experience has been limited to driving along the rather drab landscape on the New Jersey Turnpike, I can understand why you might not have the most favorable impression of the Garden State. There are plenty of rolling hills and open spaces in the northern tier of the state, and the beach area is a great place to visit. There really are some very nice areas of the state. We spent many summer vacations at the New Jersey beach and still like to visit Cape May, a charming, picturesque Victorian ocean town.

I grew up on the property of the Seeing Eye Breeding Division, which was affectionately referred to as the Puppy Farm by many of us locals. The Seeing Eye's goal, according to their mission statement, is to "enhance the independence, dignity, and self-confidence of people who are blind, through the use of specially trained Seeing Eye dogs." The Seeing Eye Breeding Division was located just outside the quaint little town of Mendham, NJ, complete with numerous clapboard and brick houses, specialty shops, and restaurants in a pastoral setting. Mendham is small town Americana at its finest.

Much of a Walt Disney movie featuring the Seeing Eye was filmed right where we lived. It was great fun. Called "Atta Girl, Kelly," the movie was released in 1967. It was about a German shepherd pup being trained to become a Seeing Eye dog and the positive impact she had on each of her three masters.

I even got a small part in the movie as a stand-in. Walt Disney did not want to bring the boy who played Kelly's 4-H owner across country to shoot the scenes that were being filmed at the Seeing Eye, so I got to do those. My total screen time probably amounted to less than 30 seconds and the filming was done from so far away you couldn't possibly tell it was me. But, of course, I thought I was kind of a big deal.

You may have noticed that each child in our family has a first name that begins with a "J." Naming an entire litter of puppies this way was customary for tracking purposes. So, we became my mom and dad's "J" litter.

As kids, we knew that some very important service was being provided where we lived, but mostly, we knew we had an ample supply of soft, furry, warm puppies waiting for us anytime we wanted to visit the kennels.

My father had the privilege of being the first director of the Seeing Eye Breeding Division. My parents told us the first dogs they had were military dogs used in World War II. Suffice it to say some of the early years were a bit challenging and frightening. My mom told us about a time when her kerchief was all that saved her when an aggressive dog latched onto her throat.

Mr. Morris Frank, who was blind, and his guide dog Buddy

were the famed duo who really started the Seeing Eye. Another movie, entitled "Love Leads the Way," was their story. Mr. Frank had read an article about guide dogs being employed by blinded World War I veterans. After having completed training in Switzerland, Mr. Frank arrived in New York City to demonstrate the ability of his guide dog. As a skilled team working together, he and Buddy safely navigated a dangerous city street crossing to the amazement of a large group of media gathered to record the event. From this humble beginning, the Seeing Eye was born. I am proud to report that I just saw recently that the Seeing Eye Dog has been named the official state dog for New Jersey.

Adjoining our house, we had over one hundred acres of woods, fields, hills, streams and waterfalls to explore. We had ample space for baseball, softball, kickball, and football, which meant our house was the gathering place for the neighborhood kids. When winter arrived, we had absolutely epic hills for sledding. The place really was "kidtopia."

In addition to our pet German Shepherds, Juan and then Justin (the J thing again), we accumulated quite a menagerie of critters over the years. At different times there was Jinny, the beagle; JiJi, the toy poodle; and Napoleon, the basset hound. I am not sure why he didn't have a name that began with a "J." It could be because his behavior did not justify this prestigious honor. He was small and mischievous, just like his namesake.

We had a number of dogs over the years, which, I suppose is not that unusual. Yes, but what about the other pets we had? We had a goat named Bambie and a raccoon named Whiskers. My cousin Tom was on his way to visit us one day and saw baby Whiskers on the side of the road, having gotten separated from his family. Tom picked him up, put him safely in his coat pocket, and delivered him to my mom. My mother, having never met a baby animal that she didn't want to rescue, bottle-fed and nurtured Whiskers until he became a healthy, young raccoon. Whiskers, of course, recognizing a good thing when he had it, stayed with us for three to four years.

Living with children who were more than ready to play with him and feed him treats, he grew strong and healthy, achieving a weight of about 50 pounds. He was a rather large raccoon, perhaps just a bit on the chubby side. He was a fun pet. As you may know, raccoons will put their food in water prior to eating. We loved to tease Whiskers by giving him sugar cubes, and of course providing a bowl of water to make sure he washed them first. Our poor confused raccoon could simply not comprehend where his treat had disappeared to. He would search frantically with his eyes and paws for it after it dissolved.

Looking back, one of the more comical things about having this unique collection of pets was that we really didn't consider it unusual. The entire group of animals got along, joined us in all our activities, and had the run of the house. In the afternoon, as our school bus would approach our stop, we would see the whole band of animals patiently waiting at the bottom of the driveway for us. When we got off the bus, we would be mobbed by this enthusiastic group anxious to begin whatever after-school excitement might be in store for them.

I remember my grandmother, Nan, told me that when she would take my sister in a stroller for a walk, Whiskers went too. More than one concerned motorist stopped to let her know she was being followed by a raccoon! I guess we just figured everyone had a pet raccoon and goat and didn't really think it was anything special.

You have probably figured out by now that I am an animal lover. They have always had a special place in my life. I have often thought a good way to measure a person's true character is to watch them interact with an animal or a young child. For our adult interactions, we are often in character, depending on whom we may be trying to impress. But our interactions with an animal or child are pure, usually free of pretense and provide better insight into our real personality.

I believe that God gave us animals to serve as companions and helpers on our journey through life.

But ask the animals, and they will teach you, or the birds in the sky, and they will tell you; or speak to the earth, and it will teach you, or let the fish in the sea inform you. Which of all these does not know that the hand of the LORD has done this? In his hand is the life of every creature and the breath of all mankind (2 Job 10-7).

As children we really did have a pretty idyllic existence. I can remember when our behavior would indicate we were taking it all for granted, my dad would remind us of how fortunate we were. Of course, he was right, but we certainly didn't know it back then. All of us do now!

→3←

LIFE, LOVE, AND CHURCH

Do everything in love (1 Corinthians 16:14).

My mother was raised in the quaint little town of Madison, New Jersey, and was a member of the Catholic faith. She did quite well in school and was offered an academic scholarship to college. I remember her telling me that her parents would not pay the costs that weren't covered by the scholarship, so she ended up not going to college. In all fairness to my grandparents, remember this was during the 1940s and according to them, "a woman's place was in the home."

Undeterred by this disappointment, my mom did not let the lack of a college degree hold her back. She was a smart lady and managed to do quite well in her work career. My mom was also a very passionate and caring person. She was of Irish heritage and had the red hair and freckles to match her land of origin. She could be outspoken and opinionated. She was like a mama bear and used her strength of character to protect us on more than one occasion.

I very much take after my mother, and many of her personality traits have proven to be of benefit to me, although I had a pretty bad temper when I was younger and was prone to outbursts. I can remember my parents threatening to remove me from my Little League team because of my temper. I was a pitcher and had a terrible habit of yelling at my fielders when they made an error. Of course, I learned that my outbursts didn't help them very much when another ball was hit to them. I had made them too nervous to field the ball! So, I learned an important lesson in teamwork and sportsmanship.

My mother was completely devoted to her children. She provided us with unconditional love and made each of us feel special. The time and effort that she spent making our birthday parties and holiday activities special was incredible. My mom worked countless hours on our homemade Halloween costumes. She would sew at the dining room table and assemble them on the living room floor. I know that is a little hard to imagine today when it is so easy to pop into a store to buy a costume or purchase one online. We consistently won the costume contest held at the nearby Ralston Firehouse. I cannot verify this but was told we won so much that we were banned from future competitions at one point.

My father spent his childhood in New Brunswick, New Jersey. He lived on the working farm that was part of the Rutgers University Agriculture Program. My grandfather served as the maintenance director for the farm. Dad shared many stories of the wonderful times he had growing up on the farm. My dad was a devout Christian and was raised in the Lutheran faith.

He served in the Navy during World War II aboard the destroyer escort USS Cronin. As is fairly typical of the Greatest Generation, he spoke very reluctantly and humbly about his war experience. I didn't realize until adulthood that he was in constant danger during the war because the job of a destroyer escort was to accompany Merchant Marine vessels and engage in anti-submarine warfare.

Although he was a Lutheran, my dad converted to Catholicism prior to my parent's marriage. He was somewhat of a quiet and introverted person, and he relished the role of being a father. According to my mom, during a time when it was not considered a man's job, he changed our diapers and gave us baths.

He was actively involved in our lives and activities. He participated in Boy Scouts and YMCA Indian Guides with my brothers.

He pitched baseballs to me for batting practice, threw me a football, and shot baskets with me. He and my Uncle Charlie always took my cousin Kevin and me to a New York Yankee baseball game for our birthdays. We used to go to doubleheader games on Sundays, which meant a total of about six hours of baseball. Of course, Kevin and I were thrilled by this. But I am quite sure that for my dad, who really was not much of a sports fan, it must have been a very long day.

My father was a nature lover and instilled in all his children an admiration and appreciation of God's creation. I am so incredibly grateful for this gift as it has served to be an integral part of my Christian faith. "For since the creation of the world God's invisible qualities-his eternal power and divine nature-have been clearly seen, being understood from what has been made . . ." (Romans 1:20). I was blessed to have wonderful, loving, and nurturing parents. I hope this book proves to be a suitable tribute to honor them.

My grandmother Nan was also very influential in my childhood years. She was a devout Catholic, and I remember her attending church without fail every Sunday. She would often participate in the Catholic custom of having a mass said on behalf of a family member or lighting a candle in the church for a special family member she was praying for. I also remember she played Bingo at her church and won regularly. I very much looked forward to sharing her winnings, which were usually chocolate candy bars for the grandchildren.

Sadly, she was the only surviving grandparent when I was a child. She was the matriarch of the family. She was revered and loved. Nan was a very caring and nurturing presence, spending a lot of her time at our house. I hope you too have been fortunate enough to have shared the love of a special grandparent.

The very first memory I can recall in life was when I was around three years of age. I remember being in Nan's bedroom, lying on her chest while she sang to me. As children at that age are prone to do, I can remember asking her to sing the same song over and over again. "K-K-K-Katy" was my favorite:

"K-K-K-Katy, oh beautiful Katy
you're the only girl that I adore . . ."

This was a popular World War I era song written by Canadian American composer Geoffrey O'Hara over 100 years ago! I am curious to see how many readers recall that song. It is kind of an "old test" for you! The song has additional special meaning for me because my Nan was named Catherine, and my daughter is named after her. Both have used the nickname of Katie.

During my childhood, we attended St. Joseph's Catholic Church as a family every Sunday. As was customary at that time, I remember getting dressed up in a coat and tie as did my brothers and dad while my mom and sister wore their Sunday Best dresses to go to church.

I have very pleasant memories of church, and I recall the church community being very warm and friendly. I especially remember the ladies auxiliary having bake sales after church. I can't say for certain but suspect that promises of their donuts may have served as bargaining chips to insure my good behavior in church on more than one occasion.

Another vivid memory I have of this time was of the head pastor, Father Joseph Gallo. I remember being a little frightened during his sermons. He was a traditional "fire and brimstone" preacher. He would consistently and passionately lecture the congregation on the need to repent for their wrongdoing and seek God's forgiveness.

In particular, I remember Father Gallo being quite distraught with the dress, hair, and conduct of the teenagers. Keep in mind, this was the 1960s, arguably one of the time periods associated with some of the greatest social upheaval in American history. So, I think his concern was probably warranted. I am confident history would show it is not uncommon for teenagers to incur the wrath of the older generation for many of the problem's society faces.

Father Gallo's approach was not completely unique for that time period. I am sure his methods may have resonated with some of the adult congregation, but as a small child, I was quite terrified. I remember cowering back into the pew and tuning him out.

There was no such thing as junior church or separate programs for the youth at that time. Having that available today for the younger crowd represents a significant step forward to effectively engage children in a Christian church service.

From ages five until nine, I attended Brookside Elementary School and have fond memories of my time there. I remember my kindergarten teacher, Ms. Darrell, who was very kind and fun. I fell in love instantly and recall proposing marriage to her.

I received my Christian education at this time by attending Confraternity of Christian Doctrine (CCD) classes at St. Joseph's. I recall that the program was held on Saturday morning, which made it particularly unappealing to me. I remember hiding in the garage sometimes with my brother Jeff until the bus that was supposed to pick us up left. We would then boldly report to my mother that the bus was early, or we were a little late getting out the door. Of course, our not getting on the bus was most definitely not our fault. However, we did attend most of the time, and I completed my CCD training at about age seven. I then received my First Holy Communion, which represents the beginning of a youth's commitment to the Catholic faith.

➤4◄

A LESSON LEARNED

It is not that I'm so smart. But I stay with the questions much longer. –Albert Einstein

It is kind of funny the things that children remember and some of the seemingly small and pretty insignificant things that make an impression on them. If you are a parent or even if you are working with children, never underestimate the importance of your role and the vital impact you can play in their development, good and bad. Even something that you might believe to be insignificant and in-consequential can have a lasting impact on a child. Be a good person and a positive role model.

As I look back on early experiences that had a profound impact on me, I am pretty sure my first important lesson in morality was provided by my dad somewhere when I was between the ages of three and four. He would often take me with him to run errands during his lunch hour. On one of these trips he took me to the hardware store in town. I picked up some loose nails from a bin and put them in my pocket. Apparently at some point later that day, my dad saw me working on one of my construction projects with some shiny new nails and asked where I got them. I con-fessed, and we took a trip back to the hardware store to return them.

I remember apologizing to the store owner and giving the nails back. It served as a very early and significant lesson and made quite an impression on me. I have never stolen another thing in my life! I

15

am so grateful my father took the time to impart this valuable life lesson. I remember wondering later how many fathers would have realized the small value of those nails and just let it go. My dad didn't and I am grateful to him for that.

I have joyful memories of this time in my life. I lived in a nice comfortable home with a family I loved and knew they loved me. In addition to neighborhood friends, I was lucky to have my cousin Kevin born just five days after me. We would alternate spending weekends at each other's houses. Kevin would come up to visit, while my sister, Joanne, would visit my cousin Kathy. The next time we would switch, and I would visit Kevin while Kathy came to our house.

Kevin and I shared a passion for sports particularly baseball. My dad constructed a backstop for us, and mom made us home-made bases with her sewing machine, and we would play constantly. Day in and day out. Scorching heat, oppressive humidity, or rain. It didn't matter. We played ball! It is no wonder that as adults both of us have suffered degenerative rotator cuff injuries to our throwing arms!

I was basically a good kid and got good grades in school. I didn't get in too much trouble except for some occasional fights and talking and joking around too much in class. I had a few rough edges that needed smoothing to become a finished product.

My family and all the relations on my mother's side were Catholic. This was something that we held with pride, and there were certainly many positive experiences and opportunities provided by our Catholic Church membership. Unfortunately, I can clearly remember being told that because we were Catholic, we would be granted eternal life in heaven, and we should pray for everyone else's salvation. Even back then, I can recall having a very difficult time accepting this, knowing that Catholics represented only a small percentage of people here on earth. I remember being particularly distressed because a number of my friends were not of the Catholic faith and would not be going to heaven. I am confident this is not part of Catholic doctrine anymore.

I believe with all my heart that what God asks most of us is to live our lives in a Christian manner and follow his commandments. In addition, we need to humbly accept his son Jesus Christ as our savior and apply his teachings. I am confident that God is not really concerned about the particular Christian church where we choose to do that.

So, why do we choose a denomination and church to begin with? I think this is a critical question and one that demands careful and reflective thought. Maybe you attend the church you grew up in, and it is simply logical that you continue to be part of it. That would make perfect sense. Maybe you like the music program at a church or maybe you chose a particular church because they have a very active youth group. But if you are choosing a new church home, make sure you select it for the right reason(s).

We need to be careful when selecting a church because inherent in our decision may be a subtle belief that this church does things right and is better. It is not uncommon for a denomination to tell its followers that they have "the truth." So, if your church does things right and has the truth, does that make other churches wrong? Can you see how this could possibly result in feelings of superiority to others who may have different beliefs? Unfortunately, we then place ourselves in a position of judgment that obviously is completely contrary to the very heart of Christianity. Some food for thought, I suppose.

People are not perfect, therefore the church is not perfect. Think about all those who Jesus came to earth to save—they include the ones on the fringe of society, the outcasts. A church by nature of its Christian mission should welcome these people. Those who are struggling should be welcomed with open arms.

Jesus was the first and best minister, and he didn't have a church. The market square was his church, as was a friend's home.

I firmly believe that a great many of the important and positive things we do as Christians don't really take place within the confines of a church building anyway. Certainly, a church provides somewhere to praise God but so do car trips, hikes, and everywhere and anywhere else you like.

We can't let a building confine our faith because we will never engage in active Christianity if we do. We will not make the world a better place just by going to church. We might not do so by being active disciples for God either, but I think we have a much better chance. The building structure is not the church. It is the people who are the church, and it is the people who are out engaging and serving others that will spread God's love and change their minds and hearts.

I am not church bashing. Historically, I think the church has done far more good than bad. I just think it is important to acknowledge that church members, like everyone else, are flawed human beings; therefore, mistakes will be made, and problems will occur.

I believe in active Christianity. I think it is important to be out in the community helping and serving others who may be in need or may be non-believers. That is what Jesus did and it was the cornerstone of his ministry. The word "Christian" appears in the New Testament (KJV) only three times, but the word "disciple" appears 273 times. I think the message is clear—it is not enough to be a Christian; we are expected to be disciples and share our faith with others.

Looking back now, I am eternally grateful to my parents for those early church experiences, including CCD. I now know that the seeds of Christianity were planted then. It was up to me to make sure they were nourished and grew.

➤5◀

CATHOLIC SCHOOL EXPERIENCES

Train up a child in the way he should go; even when he is old, he will not depart from it (Proverbs 22:6).

Nineteen sixty-three is the year that my beloved New York Yankees lost the World Series to the Los Angeles Dodgers four games to zero. Hall of Fame pitcher Sandy Koufax pitched two complete games and struck out twenty-three. Despite the Yankees losing the series, I became an avid fan, and that event began my love affair with sports that has continued to this day. In fact, my entire work career has revolved around sports. Funny, how things work sometimes!

I was hooked on baseball and then, depending on the season, also became a football and basketball fan. Back then, World Series games were played during the day, and I remember sneaking a transistor radio into school with an earphone so I could listen during school. Did you just say, "A what?" Yes, a transistor radio. Another "old test" for you!

It was also during 1963 that the St. Joseph's Parish in Mendham opened a new school for students in grades four through eight. Eventually the school would provide a full kindergarten through 8th grade program. To my dismay, I learned that St. Joseph's has now closed after 57 years. I really hope this is not a trend for Catholic schools. Catholic schools and Christian schools, in general, play a vitally important role in the education of our young people and preparing them to be morally sound, contributing members of our society.

I remember there being quite a bit of excitement about the opening of a new Catholic school. Many of my friends along with my brother Jeff and I made the transition to the new school. My older brother John was already in high school, but my sister Joanne would eventually follow us to St. Joseph's School.

St. Joseph's Church was built in 1853 and is a charming and beautiful little church. I can picture its incredibly intricate and magnificent stained-glass windows. Even now as I sit here reflecting, I can almost smell the burning incense that often filled the air inside.

The initial school faculty was provided by the Missionary Sisters of the Immaculate Conception. I am both appreciative and genuinely impressed by the nuns that taught me from 4th through 8th grade. They were very loving and patient and proved to be outstanding educators. Each grade level teacher taught all subjects consisting of English, Spelling, Math, Science, History, and Religion. We left the classroom for Music and Physical Education, which were taught by lay teachers.

I cannot imagine the workload these teachers had! Imagine preparing lessons for that many subjects daily not to mention grading homework, tests, reports, and projects. I taught for nine years and typically had to prepare for one to three subjects each night and thought that was plenty.

We didn't have a working cafeteria, so I remember my daily lunch consisted of a cheese sandwich and carton of milk. Pretty bland, huh? Yes, but once that was gone, I enjoyed the holy grail of lunch desserts: Drakes Cakes! Ring Dings, Devil Dogs, Yodels, and Funny Bones but not all in the same day of course, although back then I probably would have been thrilled by that challenge. My dessert was the envy of many of my classmates. Dad knew how to pack a lunch that would sustain a hardworking middle school student through the rigors of a tough afternoon in the classroom.

Sister Mariella was by far my favorite teacher. I know she was from South America, although I am not certain what country she called home. She called me "Diego," which I enjoyed and didn't find out until years later it was my Spanish name! I remember her smile, which she seemed to wear the entire school day. If things didn't work out with my kindergarten teacher, Ms. Darrell, I am pretty sure I would have tried to convince Sister Mariella to leave the convent and marry me.

As I mentioned earlier, I have always tended to talk a bit too much, and my time at St. Joseph's was no different. I was definitely a class clown. It was my good fortune to have had very kind and patient teachers. As a former teacher, I really believe if I had me in class, I would have kicked myself out.

One day at school, the nuns separated the fifth grade boys and girls for "The Talk." Of course, every kid that age knew about and looked forward to "The Talk." "The Talk" began with a statement about "now that you are older." As you can imagine, a room of pre-adolescent boys fell completely silent and leaned forward in their desk chairs, anxiously waiting for the next words to be said. As it turned out, during our Talk, the boys were told that since we were getting older, we should start using deodorant. The girls were told about menstruation. Needless to say, both the boys and girls were incredibly disappointed.

I remember getting in a few fights during my time at St. Joseph's. Most of the time it seems that we were able to settle our differences without adult intervention and move on without any additional fighting. We really did not have problems with bullying. I did have my knuckles rapped with a ruler by Principal Sister Bonfilia more than once and probably deserved it more than that. When I did fight, I was punished at home as well, and I know my parents never questioned the school about how they handled the situation.

I know this comment may sound a bit outdated, but I will take my chances. I truly think as adults we are too quick to intervene in our children's problems. Unfortunately, it seems we jump into many situations too quickly and blindly to protect our children. If your child got into a fight, is it possible they instigated it? If they aren't starting every basketball game or didn't get an A on a math test, it is okay; maybe they need more practice or need to study better. Help them deal with the disappointment and move on.

There is value in giving children a chance to work through their failures. I realize that it was a private school and a different time, but I think allowing us to settle our own disputes helped us. Conflict resolution is a valuable skill and cannot be learned if children are never given an opportunity to practice it.

I am trying to be as honest as possible regarding my school experiences. While I am not proud that I was a class clown or got in fights, it is a part of who I was. I was not perfect then and I am by no means perfect today. Don't panic if you are the parent of a child like I was. Be patient and love your child just like God loves us despite our shortcomings.

I found my first girlfriend while attending St. Joseph's. Beth Ann and I "dated" from fourth through eighth grade. Okay, we didn't really date. In actuality, I was too scared to talk to her. This is a fact that my granddaughter finds quite amusing and enjoys teasing Papa about his first girlfriend. We were permitted one slow dance at each of the school dances, and I always danced with her so in my mind she was my girlfriend. We used to line those dance dates up months in advance. I remember the nuns would walk around during the slow dance and make sure they could see daylight between the dancing couples. If you were dancing too close, you could expect a nun in stealth ninja mode to sneak up and perform a "karate chop" that would force you to separate.

Daily recess consisted of kickball day after day for the boys and jump rope for the girls. Amazingly, it really is all I remember anyone doing, but apparently, we didn't get tired of it. We played our games in the parking lot every chance we got no matter the weather conditions. There were a lot of torn pants and skinned knees, but we kept on playing.

As I said, we were provided with a music class. We performed numerous concerts for the parents and community. In fact, we produced a vinyl album of patriotic songs as a school fundraiser. I think because I had a tendency to misbehave, I was selected for a solo. I suspect they felt they could keep a better eye on me that way. I know it wasn't for my singing voice. I sang "My Country 'Tis of Thee." Honestly, I had a very nasal tone that produced something sounding like a Boston accent. If you closed your eyes it wasn't hard to imagine the song was being sung by a young John F. Kennedy.

The school was strict, which I didn't care for at the time, but in hindsight now realize it was a good thing. Later, as I began raising my own children, I began to resurrect and apply those Catholic values I had learned. Setting reasonable boundaries through discipline obviously helps a child learn right and wrong and enables them to develop a healthy respect for others too. It is so important for children to learn to look beyond themselves and respect the needs of others.

We were required to wear uniforms which, of course at the time, I failed to see the benefit of. Boys wore gray or navy pants, a white shirt, and a tie. The girls wore navy, gold, and green plaid skirts, a white shirt, and what I am told was called a "cross tie" around their necks. If we were cold, we could wear a navy sweater. I do recall that the girls had to have their top button secured and when they knelt their skirt had to touch the floor. Disciplinary action was taken if there was a dress code violation. Having a dress code saved parents the expense of an extensive school wardrobe and eliminated any fashion competition. Not a bad thing. I know dress codes are still common in private schools and even some public schools have adopted them.

Father Gallo was the parish priest when I started school at St. Joseph. I remember he had the responsibility of personally handing out report cards. If you can imagine, he would stand in the front of the class, look over each student's report card, and make comments on their successes and failures. We were all mortified! Fortunately, I got good grades during this time, so I escaped his wrath. However, I do remember him addressing some of my poor underachieving classmates. It went something like this. Shaking his head and exhaling in despair he would say: "Well, son, your parents are going to be pretty disappointed—an F in Spelling, and I see you talk too much in class. What are we going to do about this?" Can you imagine anything like that happening today? Father Gallo was strict, but he really was a great guy once you got to know him.

I was an altar boy during my time at St. Joseph's as were most of my friends. I would often assist Father Gallo when he performed the church service. Being an altar boy was considered an honor and if I remember correctly was reserved for boys in seventh and eighth grades. I can remember the pressure of assisting the priest during service, knowing your friends were in the audience critiquing your performance. One of our responsibilities was to ring a bell at key points during the service. I can recall the embarrassment of forgetting to ring the bell or ringing it late. It was tough facing your classmates in school the next day after such an epic failure.

At the conclusion of each school year, Father Gallo would take us to Palisades Amusement Park. Those of you who grew up in northern New Jersey, New York, or Connecticut during this time will fondly recall this park located on the picturesque cliffs overlooking the Hudson River and the New York skyline. Here is another old test. Do you remember their advertising jingle? "ride the coaster, get cool in the waves in the pool, you'll have fun, so come on over."

We were fortunate to be part of the St. Joseph's community, which provided a sense of belonging and support for us. The school did an excellent job of preparing us for high school. Along with so many other students and parents of the local community, I owe them a significant debt of gratitude.

As Jesus came to serve, the nuns and priests who taught and guided us followed and applied his example. Looking back, my Catholic School experience was an extremely important time in my development. The seeds of Christianity had now developed some roots.

⇒6⇐

SURVIVAL MODE

Being challenged in life is inevitable, being defeated is optional. —*Roger Crawford*

As I said earlier, I had a magical childhood. I was extremely fortunate to live in a loving home with a loving family. We really had an idyllic existence. However, things can change quickly, and life for us did just that.

Prior to his aneurysm rupture, my dad had experienced periodic debilitating headaches for years and had been to see the doctor numerous times. In fact, I can remember just a few days before his aneurysm ruptured, he was at one of my baseball games and had to lie down under a tree near the field because of a severe headache. Although my dad had been to the doctor and testing was performed, at that time, the technology simply did not exist to properly diagnose the cause of his headaches.

If my dad had this problem today, it would have been diagnosed by an MRI or CAT scan, and a surgery would have been performed prior to rupture. Life certainly would have been different.

It is interesting looking back and realizing how blinded by optimism our family was. My father had suffered major brain trauma and somehow, we all expected things would eventually be the same. We were all convinced our family life would be as it had always been.

The changes in my dad were subtle in many ways, and this really made it even more difficult. I remember thinking that maybe it would have been easier if he had been more disabled or incapacitated. There would have been something obvious, reminding us he was different. Maybe if he had appeared different, we would have treated him differently. I am quite embarrassed to share that each member of our family has admitted thinking that maybe it would have been better for him and us if he had not survived the surgery.

As it was, my dad looked the same and, in some ways, acted the same. But he wasn't the same. For example, he had always been somewhat quiet and easy going, but now he was passive with no motivation. There were now three teenage boys in the house who desperately needed direction and control. While my mom had usually been the disciplinarian, my dad was at least involved in the past. Suddenly, he was just a passive observer. As a result, we were more out of control, and my mom grew more and more frustrated and upset.

Physically, my dad did return to normal, but there were definite mental and emotional changes. The aneurysm had been in the frontal lobe of the brain, which is responsible for controlling things like judgment, decision making, problem solving, and emotions. Not surprisingly, all these things were affected. He really ended up a shell of his former self.

I do realize that what my family experienced is small compared to the tragedy and challenges others face and overcome. We are all aware of countless stories of people who despite suffering horrible personal tragedy, have managed to rise above the situation and thrive. Sadly, our family was just not able to do that. I sincerely wish we had been.

I have experienced a variety of conflicting emotions over the years. I certainly displayed misplaced anger toward my father. I have been angry at myself because of it and the fact that I didn't handle it better. I have been embarrassed knowing that the situation I dealt with pales in comparison with what many others have been faced with and overcome. I loved God for sparing my father and returning him to our family. I have also been angry at God because he was not the same father after his aneurysm.

To compound the stress of the struggle we were engaged in, we stopped going to church and pretty much withdrew from the church community. My sister Joanne who was going to be entering fifth grade at St. Joseph's was pulled from the school and began attending public school. We were never given a reason for these changes, but I guess my mother felt as if we didn't get the support we should have had from the church and school community. It may have also been an indication of her rejecting her faith as well.

I realize now there was a very strange disconnect occurring at this time as well. We were constantly being told how lucky we were that my dad survived and how wonderful God was to bring him back to us. We knew that and we were grateful, but he wasn't the same person—this wasn't our dad. He looked like him and somewhat acted like him, but he was different. That made it really hard for all of us, including my father. We were grateful but angry. We were a jumble of conflicted emotions.

I do know my mom blamed God for what happened to our family. I can remember, she would ask, "How could God do this to us?" I was fourteen years old at the time and was in no way prepared to provide any kind of meaningful answer. I do recall saying to my mom that "God only gives us what we can handle." I think this was really little more than a desperate plea of hope on my part for my mom to find the strength to guide us through these hard times. Sadly, my mom built a wall to protect us. Our family desperately needed the love and support of the community, but we withdrew into a shell to survive.

In reality, if God does give us more than we can handle, it is so we can turn our attention toward him. Our struggles can strengthen us. The author, JRR Tolkein, suffered the devastation of losing both of his parents by the time he was twelve years old. He fought in World War I and experienced the horrors of war and the death of beloved friends. He became a professor at Oxford University in England and was a devout Christian. His books, *The Hobbit* and the *Lord of the Ring* trilogy are considered among the most popular books ever written.

Rebekah Gregory suffered abuse as a child by her father, an evangelical minister. She and her five-year-old son attended the 2013 Boston Marathon to support a friend who was running. The blasts of terrorists' bombs packed with nails and screws went off only a few feet away from where they were standing. Her legs took the brunt of the force, enabling her to protect her son from certain death. After eighteen surgeries and sixty-five procedures, her left leg was finally amputated. She certainly has had reason to be angry and turn away from her faith. Instead she has written a memoir that describes the peace we experience when we learn to trust God with our lives, even the most terrifying and difficult parts. She has also started a ministry designed to inspire and help others who have experienced hardship.

Joni Eareckson Tada became a quadriplegic as the result of a diving accident. She has overcome this tragedy and risen above her disability. She is an author, speaker, and radio host. She has developed a ministry dedicated to presenting the hope of the Gospel to people affected by disability through programs and outreaches around the world. Her program also trains and mentors people with disabilities to apply their gifts of leadership and service in their churches and communities.

In the Bible, look at the hardships poor Job was willing to endure yet remained steadfast in his faithfulness to God. For months he endured open sores covering his entire body. His entire wealth and livelihood were wiped out in one afternoon. He suffered the tragedy of losing seven sons and three daughters. Yet, during all of his troubles, he remained stubbornly faithful to God.

These are only a few stories about those who have overcome

adversity through the love and grace of God. There are countless others, many of which I am sure you are aware of. God made us and understands us better than we understand ourselves. And he certainly understands and can identify with our pain and anguish. He sent his Son to save us and watched him ridiculed and tortured. Jesus suffered a horribly painful death. Crucifixion was a carefully crafted technique to produce maximum pain. God understands our suffering.

We ran away from God when we should have been running toward him. Had we turned to God instead of away from him, I am confident we would have managed much, much better.

I was always very close to my mom. My siblings would tease me about being her favorite, but looking back, I might have been. Our personalities were very similar, we understood each other, and we were very close. She was the one I could always talk to. Unfortunately, because of this, I very much identified with her so I too was angry at God.

My mom's relationship with my dad became strained, and I sided with my mom and became angry at my dad. I began treating him disrespectfully and did not provide the love and compassion he deserved.

Each member of our family was affected in their own way. Looking back, our family really needed counseling to help us work through this traumatic time period. I suppose considering the time period when this occurred, it is most likely counseling simply wasn't offered to us. Emotional health issues were not addressed the way they are today. That was an era when you were more expected to "tough it out" or "just deal with it." And I suppose there are times when that can be done. This, however, was not one of them.

Amazingly, I do remember that we never really discussed any of it. We never sat down and talked about what had happened, the changes facing all of us, and the adjustments we would all need to make. Also, I never remember any of us talking about our frustrations as we all struggled to move forward.

I know that at one time our family was well respected in the community and considered to be an exemplary Christian family. Sadly, after my father's brain aneurysm I don't think that was the case. There was a significant element of dysfunction in our family then.

I clearly remember one incident that sadly reflects the way I treated my father during this time. We were at one of my baseball games, and the base umpire didn't show up. So, my dad being the good guy he was, volunteered to do this. During the game, there was a close play at first base, and he gave the upward thumb motion indicating that the runner was out but yelled "safe." A rather heated discussion ensued among the coaches and my father about what the exact call was. Fans in the stands also weighed in rather strongly with their opinions as well. Now, keep in mind my father was doing us a huge favor by agreeing to serve as the base umpire. However, in the eyes and mind of a sensitive and self-absorbed adolescent, this was an unpardonable mistake. I remember being very angry and embarrassed about my dad's umpiring error. How could he have done this to me? How could he humiliate me in front of my teammates and all their parents? I must reluctantly admit that situation was fairly typical of how I felt about my dad at that time.

My dad was an early riser, so he would always be up and in the kitchen when I was eating breakfast. On the other hand, I have never met a morning that I really liked. I can remember without fail every morning when I would pour my orange juice, my dad would remind me to "swish it around," meaning I should shake the container to distribute the pulp. I remember biting my tongue so that I wouldn't respond with anger. And do you know what? To this day when I get my orange juice in the morning, I shake the container. And we even buy no pulp orange juice! Now, I laugh when I shake the container and think of my dad. I have wished many, many times that I could turn back the clock and undo some of those hurtful things I thought, said, and did.

At this point in my writing, it is Father's Day and as I do every Father's Day and Mother's Day, I spend time reflecting on memories of my parents. Interestingly, it occurred to me today for the first time that although I was closest to my mother, the earliest memories of my parents are mostly of my father. I had never realized that before. He is the one who taught me to swim and ride a bike. He was the one who taught me to throw and hit a baseball, catch and throw a football, and shoot a basketball. I am really looking forward to being reunited with my dad in heaven. I can't wait to see him. There is so much I need to tell him.

⇒7⇐

TEENAGE TRIBULATIONS

Teenager- "When you are too young to do half the things you want, and too old to do the other half"- *Author unknown.*

I was about to start ninth grade at West Morris High School. This was a very large regional high school at the time that eventually became three schools. It was a bit of culture shock for me having come from a small private Catholic school. West Morris was a huge and intimidating school. Starting there in the fall following the summer of my father's brain aneurysm was a perfect storm for disaster.

Obviously, the transition to high school can be a period of adjustment and a difficult time for any teen and this combined with the emotional upheaval our family was experiencing made my 9th grade year my most challenging school year. I began to adopt a rebellious attitude at home and at school. Of course, I was desperate to create an image to match my defiant attitude, so I dressed in jeans, a jean jacket, and boots pretty much every day. To further cultivate my image, I began to smoke. I think back now about having done that, and it is almost incomprehensible for me. I consider smoking a pretty disgusting and unhealthy habit.

We had a small apartment above our garage we called "the cottage," and this became our place to hang out, drink, and smoke. My brother Jeff and I took turns throwing parties. In hindsight the only good thing was that everyone who came to the parties slept over, so no one was on the road driving drunk. Not to say I didn't drink and drive during this time, because I did. Unfortunately, my friends and I had no problem getting served at a number of local bars and restaurants and took full advantage of it. I drove home drunk on more than one occasion.

Not to excuse my behavior, but keep in mind it was a different time and the laws that existed to prohibit minors from consuming alcohol were pretty lax. The drunk driving laws that did exist were rather vague. Sometimes, we would cut school and travel into New York City to drink. We had a favorite place called "Steak and Brew" that provided you with all the beer you could drink while you were dining. We would buy hamburgers, eat very slowly, and drink a lot of beer. I am quite sure they had not thought about teenage boys in their business plan. Steak and Brew eventually went out of business, and we would joke that we were the reason why.

I am not sharing these things with pride. To be honest, I am quite embarrassed by much of what I have told you. But I am bringing these things up so that you have an honest idea of who I was and what I was doing. For some of you, I hope it helps you identify with my story. When I look back, I thank God that I did not get badly injured or killed doing those things, and I am equally grateful that I did not hurt or kill someone else.

I tried out for the basketball team during my ninth grade year and got cut which resulted in a deeper commitment to rebel. I remember I wouldn't touch a basketball for months after that happened. I was so angry; I didn't try out for the baseball team which, in hindsight, is rather shocking since it was my favorite sport, and I was actually good at it.

Amazingly, I didn't get into any really bad trouble at school, although my grades were pretty poor that year. I was disrespectful, angry, and hurting. As I said earlier, I have always talked a lot and joked around, but then I became sarcastic and mean.

If you recall, earlier I said I would not have wanted me in class if I were my teachers at St. Joseph's. Now, I probably would have considered a career change if I had me in class as a ninth grader.

I remember how my mom, in a very cunning and skillful mom sort of way, got me to stop smoking. She smelled smoke on my jacket and asked if I had been smoking. Of course, I denied it but when pressed further on the matter, admitted that I had been. She was a smoker at the time and asked if I would like to have a cigarette with her. I told her "no way." I mean what fun would smoking with my mom be? She made me realize I really didn't like cigarettes after all. Obviously, I didn't enjoy the experience of smoking that much if I wouldn't smoke with her. I was only smoking to impress my friends and create a tough guy image.

Another thing my mom helped with was getting me away from the group of friends I was hanging out with. A new family had moved close to us, and one day she called and asked if their son, John, a year older than me would like to go to the mall with us. He agreed and we soon became best friends.

I am sure like you, there were so many small things my parents did to help me that I took for granted or completely overlooked if I recognized them at all. They seemed so small and insignificant at that time. I didn't realize until years later how important and helpful they were. Indeed, youth is wasted on the young!

I was blessed to have my mom. I understand why she was angry about what happened to my dad, and I forgive her. Her world had been turned upside down. She was completely overwhelmed by our new reality. My dad was unable to resume many of the previous roles he had performed, so she really had to do a lot more. Eventually she had to find a full-time job because my dad was unable to perform his job duties satisfactorily and had to resign. She had only worked part time before that. She found a job as a credit manager with an oil company where she continued to work for a little more than twenty years.

We had to leave our home because the house at the Seeing Eye was part of the benefits that came with my father's job. As you can imagine, leaving the only home we had ever known was incredibly upsetting. We had to leave our friends and the town we grew up in as well.

As I mentioned earlier, my dad would sometimes tell us how spoiled we were and didn't appreciate what an amazing place and existence we had in Mendham. Of course, we soon realized how right he was.

Since the house in Mendham came with my father's job, my mother had very little money to serve as a down payment on a new one. However, my mother was able to work out a generous settlement with the Seeing Eye, and we moved to a new house in Morris Plains, NJ. The Seeing Eye always treated my family well. They are a first-class organization.

The new house was on about a ½ acre lot located right along a busy highway. This was in complete contrast to the 100-acre farm located along a quiet country road when we lived in Mendham. My mother deserves a tremendous amount of credit for finding us a nice place to live, but it was never home. For many years, I was unable to drive past our old house in Mendham; it was just too painful.

It is amazing the complete confidence and blind faith children place in their parents. In this case it was just my mother, but still we knew she would come through for us. Although we were older and as teenagers tried to act older than we were, we still needed protection. We couldn't comprehend all that was happening. We just assumed she would take care of us now like she always had, and everything would be fine. At least I know this was what I was thinking. I am sure we had to be somewhat aware of the challenges being faced, but I imagine we were also in denial about it as well.

Of course, we had a big party the night before we moved. Unfortunately, pretty much the entire town showed up. Many of our close friends who cared about us and wanted to show their support came to the party, but a lot of uninvited guests more than eager to party showed up as well. The party was a disaster. There were some fights. At some point during the party, someone got the keys to my dad's car and smashed into the corner of one of the kennel buildings. There was a ton of drunken teenagers. It was complete chaos.

Our family had survived a major crisis but only in a superficial sense of the word. We were all struggling in our own way. You might look at the ocean on a calm day, and it may appear peaceful, but there is always the possibility of a hidden undertow that could pull you under. On the surface, I think to most people our family appeared to be doing fine, and we made every effort to create that illusion. But we were all struggling to keep our heads above water. We were still trying to make sense of what happened to our father and how it affected our lives.

There is no question I was affected tremendously by my father's brain aneurysm. I described some of this earlier and some of the impact was yet to come. I had said earlier that the seeds of Christianity which had been sown began to take root in Catholic School. They were now in desperate need of a good watering.

I have shared with you how this experience affected me, and I thought it best if I let my brothers and sister tell you in their own words how they were affected. Following are their stories.

John: When I was much younger, my dad and I used to go for walks in the woods at our house in Mendham. I'd be on his shoulders, and he'd point out what he took to be fox holes. We'd look at old fences, some so old that barbed wire ran through the middle of trees and tumbled down foundations. He looked at circular piles of stone and imagined former Indian villages. I'm sure he made some of it up! I fondly recall him raking up leaf piles for us to jump in. As I got older, dad was always there to help with my ill-conceived projects which ranged from underground tunnels to rather tall log towers I secured with rope.

Dad was kindly and always reaching out to people that he saw as needing help. He was very civic-minded. The fact that he was always making calls in the community through the 4H program, or to different merchants convinced me that he was a person to be respected. Dad was very involved with the Boy Scouts and active in various funding drives, always there to help whether it was the firehouse or at the church. He was a person filled with a sense of duty, both patriotic and otherwise. Dad and his generation were giants from a world that had just ended—World War II—saviors of democracy, and of somewhat mythic stature.

Dad was somewhat stoic and always reverent. He used to go to novena's at the church and always saw God's working hand in the universe. For me one of the most familiar and at times vexing things about dad was his habit of seeing the working of God's hand everywhere from the heavens above to the depths of the sea. There was one Christmas when I was around ten when it thundered. Dad's reaction, predictably, was, "It was the birthday of a king." It deepened my own sense of awe, but it also terrified me to death.

I remember seeing him for the first time after his initial surgery following the aneurysm. He reminded me of a concentration camp survivor—wan, shaven, and out of it. As time drifted on, he was in occupational therapy and produced a small wooden stool. It made me horrified that this was my recovered father. It was common for people to congratulate us on our good fortune that he had lived. Instead it was like living with a ghost. His personality had changed dramatically.

I remember he got kicked out of the senior center for playing footsy with another guy's wife. Another time, we were eating lunch at a diner and he began saying "woof-woof" to the waitresses. Dad had always impressed me with his sense of dignity. It was all lost. He was never a jokester, but sadly had become one.

Joanne: My earliest memories are of being by my father's side. His gentle presence, his patience, his reassurance filled my life with comfort and love. He instilled in me firm values and morals, a love and respect for nature, an awe and wonder of creation and love for God.

Nature was abundant on the puppy farm, so for this little girl, toads, turtles, and tumbles were as much a part of play as Barbies, baby dolls, and bows. My first chore on the farm was coaxing the pups out of the barn for their first outdoor adventure. One by one they would follow me along the puppy trail. On our return trip, the pups would often tucker out, and we would stop in a field to rest. I will never forget the little pile of black and tan fluffs as they snuggled together for an afternoon nap.

My father and I had a special rock at Buttermilk Falls. It was here that he would share with me life sustaining scriptures: "My child, listen to me and do as I say, and you will have a long, good life. I will teach you wisdom's ways and lead you in straight paths. When you walk you won't be held back; when you run, you won't stumble. Take hold of my instructions; don't let them go. Guard them, for they are the key to life" (Proverbs 4, 10-13).

When I was in third grade, my father suffered a massive brain hemorrhage. I had gone to my cousin's for a weekend visit. Coming down the stairs one night I heard my aunt as she answered the phone, "Oh my God, John!" I knew something terrible had happened. I stayed with my cousins for the summer, but I was not told what happened to my father or when I would see him again. I remember feeling confused and so lost and lonely without him. When fall came, I was able to visit him in the hospital. His recovery was slow and challenging. When the school year began, I remember sitting beside him in our living room. I would hold his hand steady and help him as he struggled to follow the letters in my penmanship book.

Despite my invitations, my brother Jeff decided not to contribute a story of his memories of my father. He didn't give me a reason, and at first, I couldn't really understand why he would not want to do this. But the more I thought about it, I began to realize that my father's brain aneurysm and this time period may have affected him more deeply than the rest of us. Of my siblings, he is the one most like my dad. Facially, he resembles my father the most of any of us, and his personality is very similar. He also has a deep affection for animals, particularly dogs, and now works as a veterinarian.

I believe Jeff was deeply affected by my dad's aneurysm and subsequent condition following surgery. He had a very rebellious high school experience and caused my parents a significant level of stress. He, like many other teenagers at the time, was heavily into partying. Alcohol and drugs were readily available. Fortunately, most of his use consisted of marijuana and not harder drugs.

I do remember one time when he was confronted in our driveway by someone with a gun looking for money. This was typical of some of the people he was associating with at that time. There was also a night in jail on another occasion.

Fortunately, he began taking karate lessons and the discipline and training time required to be successful served as a positive substitute for his other less desirable recreational pursuits. He eventually got his black belt and became a karate instructor. Although exasperated, my parents were patient and continued to love and support him. Eventually, he did reward their patience and turned his life around.

In time, Jeff completed his college degree and eventually got his chiropractic license, and then his veterinary license. I am proud of him and all he has accomplished.

⇢8⇠

LOST AND HURTING

Trust in the Lord with all of your heart, lean not on your own understanding but acknowledge him in all your ways and he will direct your path (Psalm 3:5-6).

This is absolutely my favorite Bible verse. My daughter wrote it on a small message board in our kitchen when she was about ten years old and over twenty years later, it is still there. I find this to be the Bible verse that I need often. It has been my go-to verse when I am upset or anxious. It is my reminder to relax and trust God.

At the end of my freshman year at West Morris High School, I met Carol, my first girlfriend, and I experienced my first real kiss. Again, one of those life moments you can recall in detail. We dated through the summer and the next year and eventually broke up. She was good to me and for me. I began to grow up a bit.

During this time, my best friend John drowned while rafting on the Colorado River. I served as an altar boy and a pall bearer at his funeral service. I can remember well visiting his house after the service and seeing his mother dressed in a black dress, sitting quietly in a chair looking so sad and lost. Also, I remember for the first time in a long time thinking about God. I struggled to make sense of what had happened to my friend. I couldn't understand why God allowed him to die so young. He had so much of life ahead of him. Why would God allow my best friend to die? If God was loving and caring, how could he have allowed this to happen and why would he put his family in pain like that? I remember struggling with my friend's death and questioning my fragile faith even more. Obviously, my friend's death was devastating. It hurt and did set me back, but I was starting to grow.

In 1970, the new Mendham High School opened. It was much smaller and more intimate than West Morris. But if I am being completely honest, it was pretty ugly from the outside. I am probably understating that. Actually, it was hideous. I imagine an architect was trying to make a bold statement but failed miserably! The exterior had dark brick and black windows, and to make the building appearance even more objectionable, there was orange trim as well. It was affectionately called "The Factory." The building may have fit in an industrial park; but, in quaint, historic Mendham, it did not. Fortunately, the high school building was hardly visible from the main road, so it remained hidden. At some point it received a much-needed facelift and looks much more attractive today. One nice thing about the new school was it was much smaller and more intimate. It felt much more comfortable, and I was happy to be there.

I began playing basketball and baseball again and hanging out with my jock friends. My behavior and grades improved. By my senior year, I was getting good grades and had committed to a college education. I was becoming a better person but was not a Christian yet. However, I was more comfortable with myself and began treating people with more kindness and respect.

About halfway through my junior year, I met Maureen. She was pretty, smart, and kind. This was my first experience with real love, and the only thing that has exceeded it in intensity has been my love for my wife of over forty years.

Maureen's family was Catholic, and I attended church with them occasionally, still not enough to really make any kind of difference in my world view. We dated through the remainder of high school and my freshman year of college. She was an excellent student and at that time, much more academically motivated than I was. Looking back, I was still immature and insecure, and I think I was threatened by this. I was looking for someone who was more interested in settling down and starting a family after college graduation. We broke up toward the beginning of the fall semester of my sophomore year.

With my wife's permission, I managed to reconnect with her a few years back. She is now on the faculty of Indiana University Medical School and is an assistant director of a cancer research lab. I was really happy to find out that she had accomplished so much and has had a good life. I wish her continued success and happiness. She was a very important part of my life and helped me grow more than she knows.

After high school graduation, I attended Lock Haven University and majored in Health, Physical Education and Recreation (HPER). For the first time in my life, I took school seriously and studied.

In the winter of my sophomore year, I was working out in preparation for the upcoming baseball season and got an extremely painful case of shin splints. I couldn't walk without a limp. My friends told me to go to the trainer. I didn't know exactly who the trainer was or what he did, but I took my friends' advice.

I met someone who would end up changing my career path and life—the late David Tomasi. Although I know I thanked him, I am sure I never told him the significant impact he had on my life and I regret it. He was the school athletic trainer and a faculty member in the school of HPER. He put me on crutches and did therapy on my shins. In time I was fine and ready to play baseball.

In class one day, Mr. Tomasi announced that the school would be offering a nationally accredited athletic training curriculum beginning the following fall. I enrolled in the program and was a member of the program's first graduating class. I am now eternally grateful for a case of shin splints and thankful to Mr. David Tomasi!

Although the circumstances whereby I started my athletic training career were certainly something that at the time I looked upon as pure coincidence, I now look at it and can't help but see God's hand at work. I have worked my entire career as an athletic trainer and have enjoyed it tremendously. It has been very rewarding working with and helping people prevent and recover from their injuries. Also, I have been fortunate to develop many, many great friendships because of this work.

I finally became a serious student and got good grades in college. I did also manage to continue to have fun. I will share one of these more humorous moments with you. My friend DJ and I both had a little time on our hands one evening and decided we would take a trip down to the river and collect a bunch of bullfrogs. We had asked a female friend to meet us at the back door of the girl's dormitory next to ours later in the evening. At the appointed time we entered the dorm and let about a dozen disoriented, croaking, leaping bullfrogs go while the young ladies were brushing their teeth and performing other nightly rituals before bedtime. It was great fun! A lot of girls screaming, running, and jumping, and frogs croaking and hopping.

The college cafeteria food was, well it was food. That is about as complimentary as I can be. By my junior year I had moved off campus into an apartment with four of my friends. I decided that I was done eating in the cafeteria and would cook for myself. There was only one small flaw in my thinking—I really did not know how to cook.

For my first meal, I decided I would cook a chicken, and I did so without a recipe. I put the chicken in the oven at a temperature of about 350 degrees. I opened the oven after about 15 minutes to check on the progress of my dinner and noticed a bag with assorted chicken parts lying between my chicken's legs. This concerned me enough that I called my mom who talked me into throwing the chicken out. How was I supposed to know you needed to remove that bag before cooking? That is a rhetorical question, of course. I realized at that moment that if I didn't learn to cook, I was going to die. I am happy to report that I did improve quite a bit and am now the chief cook in our household.

My mom was an outstanding cook. After weekend visits home, she would load me up with a variety of tasty homemade treats to take back to school. My roommates would anxiously await my return, and I was happy to share with them. Unfortunately, it became apparent that one of my roommates was taking advantage of my generosity and sneaking off with a rather large share of my goodies. Now, how to catch him? I devised a terribly devious scheme. After my next trip home, I returned with a bounty of baked delights. The goodies included a plate of chocolate chip cookies that I made. Except, they weren't chocolate chips; they were pieces of Ex-Lax. The next morning one of our roommates came down with a terrible case of the stomach flu and was unable to attend classes. I had caught the culprit!

Although I changed my academic approach and became a serious student; I still hadn't grown much in any other way. I suppose I wasn't really all that different than many college students. I was selfish and self-absorbed. Many of us at that age don't have too much of a world view. We are preoccupied trying to figure ourselves out and establish our own identity. I admit, I am quite envious of those who do have a handle on their faith at that age.

I still partied a lot, streaked a little, participated in panty raids, and had fun. For those readers who were not college students in the 70s, you may have to look up campus life during that time period or talk to a grandparent to fully understand those activities.

During my freshman year, one of my close high school friends attending University of Miami committed suicide. Apparently, he had gotten heavily involved in drugs and owed someone a lot of money. I served as a pall bearer at his funeral and I remember reflecting on his death quite a bit. This tragedy hit home and it was extremely hard to make sense of. It certainly made me wonder how he could do something like this, and I think for the first time I thought some about my own mortality. It made me realize that if things had gone just a little different for me or any of my other friends; it could have been us.

I remember leaving home one time from Morris Plains and traveling Route 80 West back to school at Lock Haven in bad weather. It was raining and about 50 degrees in New Jersey and when I got to the middle of Pennsylvania it had turned into a very heavy, blinding snow. I was heading down a steep hill and at the bottom there was a bridge as the road curved to the left.

I was driving my first car, a beloved 1965 navy color Peugeot Sedan that had been handed down to me by my brothers. The minute I got on the bridge the car spun. I did two complete 360 degree turns and began praying. I have no idea how I stayed on the road. This particular area of Pennsylvania is quite desolate so if I had gone off the road and been trapped in the car or injured badly it is unlikely anyone would have found me. Also, if there had been another car nearby it would have been very possible for me to hit it since I was spinning completely out of control.

Fortunately, there were no other cars around as this was happening. After the car stopped by the grace of God, I somehow ended up back in my lane still facing west. I pulled over to the side of the road, got out, kissed the snow-covered ground and thanked God! Although I wasn't exactly a faithful Christian at the time, I still knew who to turn to when there was trouble.

→9←

SHE JUST MIGHT BE THE ONE

The future for me is already a thing of the past-you were
my first love and you will be my last. —*Bob Dylan*

At the end of my junior year of college, I met Karen at one of
her friend's parties on a Saturday night late in the spring. The next
day, I was at a home baseball game, working as a student athletic
trainer. She was there watching the game with her roommate
Carla, so I walked over to say hi.

It was an extremely cold day as is often the case when you play
baseball in north central Pennsylvania in the early spring. Karen,
seeing that I was not prepared for the weather, offered me the use
of her blanket. I thanked her and then she and Carla left.
Sometime during the week, one of my roommates ran into Karen
in the cafeteria, and she asked them to let me know she would like
her blanket back. I walked over to her dormitory, blanket in hand,
and knocked on her door. I apologized for holding her blanket
hostage and thanked her for being kind enough to share it with
me. Then I asked her on a date and kissed her goodbye.

Karen and I still disagree about the details of this encounter,
but I clearly remember kissing her. I distinctly remember walking
away and wondering about why I had just done that. Fate, destiny,
or maybe God?

We played tennis on our first date. Of course, being an HPER
major, it made perfect sense to me. Karen majored in Early
Childhood Education and was accommodating when we would

48

have sports themed dates. But she will be the first to admit that she really wasn't, and still isn't, all that interested in sports. Fortunately, she indulges my passion for them.

Interestingly enough, Karen informed me later after we had been dating awhile that she happened to be one of the girls using the bathroom the night my friend and I let the bullfrogs loose. She was not amused nearly as much as my friend and I were.

Despite the fact that she obviously lacked a good sense of humor, Karen and I dated for the remainder of our time in college all the way to graduation. She got a teaching position back in her hometown of Altoona, Pennsylvania, and I headed off to graduate school at East Stroudsburg University. As an athletic trainer, I worked a lot of weekends so Karen would usually come visit me.

After I finished graduate school, Karen spent the summer at our house in New Jersey. We both worked for a YMCA camp program that summer. It was great getting to spend that much time together, and we fell deeper in love.

As was the case in undergraduate school, God wasn't really on my radar. Again, I was growing and maturing in many ways, but not spiritually. Those roots of Christianity were now withering away.

As you may have guessed, Karen is my wife of over forty years. I loved her soon after we met and love her as much today. I am always amazed at the way God manages to bring people together. As it turned out, Karen and I had very similar childhoods. Karen's dad died from leukemia when she was five. She too was raised by a very strong, independent woman. And unfortunately like my mom, her mother, who had been very active in the church, became bitter and angry with God after her husband's death and turned away from Christianity.

Like every couple who is married for a long time, we have certainly experienced our ups and downs. At one point during our lives together, we participated in marriage counseling. I think the most valuable part of that experience was simply the fact that we both agreed to counseling, and it made both of us realize we were committed to our marriage. Let's face it, marriage is not easy, much like the other things in this life that are worth doing. There have been moments of pure joy, and there have been trying times we weren't so sure our marriage was working. Through it all, we remained committed to each other and making our marriage work.

At the risk of playing amateur marriage counselor, I will give this advice—marriage requires commitment. All of us know that but not all of us remain committed. It isn't always pretty and often requires sacrifice and effort. If you are looking for an easier and less stressful life, stay single. But if you are willing to make some sacrifices and deal with some difficult times, the rewards of marriage are well worth the effort.

I am so proud of the life Karen and I have built together. We have three children and two grandchildren whom we love dearly. They are our joy and legacy. I really believe that there would be far fewer divorces if people honored their commitment and were willing to work through the difficult times. I certainly understand there are times when a relationship is broken beyond repair and divorce is the best option. A couple certainly shouldn't stay together if a relationship is unhealthy and unsalvageable. But I would encourage exhausting every other option before divorcing. I cannot adequately express how grateful I am to Karen for her commitment to me and our family.

Karen and I were married in September 1978 in a Catholic Church. Although I was by no means a practicing Christian at that time, my Catholic roots had an influence on our selection of churches. We settled in Oxford, Pennsylvania, close to the schools where we taught. Karen taught first grade in the Oxford Area School District, and I taught health sciences and was the athletic trainer at Lincoln University.

We bought a house in 1980 and have lived there forty years.

We live in Lancaster County, Pennsylvania, or as most call it "Amish Country" and really love it here. The rolling green landscape is adorned with beautiful farms. There are also numerous hiking and biking trails along the Susquehanna River. Because the area is largely agricultural, we have a lot of farmer's markets and an abundance of roadside stands featuring an assortment of fresh fruits, vegetables, flowers, and baked goods.

Our Amish neighbors are a unique people in that they choose to remain separate from the remainder of the population they call English. They do not use electricity and do not drive cars. They drive a buggy instead that is pulled by a horse. Most of the Amish work as farmers so wedding season is in the fall. Roads can get pretty congested depending on where the wedding for that day might be. I can recall one morning heading north into Strasburg, which is typically about a 15-minute drive. I must have passed almost 50 buggies on their way to a wedding. What was typically a 15-minute drive took me about 45 minutes because of this Amish traffic jam.

I can recall being at a girls' soccer game when I was working at Octorara High School, and the Amish farmer next door to the school had just spread liquid manure on his field. The wind was blowing just the right way, so the aroma hung over the field like a dark cloud. We were playing a team from suburban Philadelphia, and I still laugh to this day when I think about that game. Our girls of course being used to farm smells were unfazed. The girls on the other team were quite distracted, however. Many of them were attempting to play while pulling their shirts up over their noses. We had a definite home field advantage and won the game.

The Amish are a very family oriented and Christian people. Most make their living as farmers, but there are also many that work as builders, carpenters, cabinet makers and store owners. They are very reliable and diligent craftsmen. Over the years, I have had Amish put an upstairs on our house, replace our roof, and pave our driveway. There really is a lot to be admired about them, and we feel blessed to live in this unique part of the country.

Not too long after we moved into our house, we thought it would be nice to start a family. We started with a Black Labrador Retriever mix that showed up at our door. If our dog Mac was any indication of what our parenting skills would be, we were going to fail miserably. We loved him but he was spoiled terribly and not real well behaved. Our male friends used to walk into our house with their hands protecting their crotch areas. In his excitement to greet visitors, he had a terrible habit of running full speed, leaping up and striking them in that very spot. They referred to him not so affectionately as "Mac, the Crotch Hound."

Convinced that we could do better than we had with Mac, we started trying to have children. After the disappointment and heartbreak of two miscarriages, the doctor told Karen that her progesterone level was low. She was able to get pregnant but could not maintain the pregnancy. She began to take the fertility drug Clomid and after just a few months on the drug became pregnant with twins.

We were about as excited and ready as any couple could possibly be to have children. I remember my mom was equally excited. Although I am the second youngest in the family, she did not have any grandchildren yet. She used to carry a copy of the ultrasound picture around in her pocketbook and proudly display it whenever an opportunity would present itself. Our twin boys, Jeremy and Matthew, were born on November 9, 1984. We were blessed to add our daughter, Kathryn, to our family on January 11, 1988. The birth of your children is one of life's defining moments and, in our case, absolutely two of the best days of our lives.

As is the case for so many parents, having a child or in our case children also signaled the beginning of a major change in our lives. Prior to marriage most of us think primarily about just one person, ourselves. We marry and then realize there is someone else to consider. Then we have children, and we experience an exponential change in responsibility. We begin caring for a life or lives that are completely dependent on us. It was time to make some significant changes for us.

Prior to our boys arriving, we would attend church on Christmas and Easter and maybe a few other times during the year. As the boys got a little older, we began to think it was time to have them receive a Christian education. We enrolled them in a Christian pre-school and started thinking about taking them to church. I was realizing then, and it would happen again many times in my life, that the Christian values I had learned long ago were critical to my identity. Even if not necessarily in the front of my consciousness, they would resurface at important points in my life. At the time I was deciding what kind of moral education I wanted my children to have, I reverted to the values instilled in me way back in CCD and Catholic School. I wanted that for my children.

✦10✦

THE LONG ROAD HOME

Listen to advice and accept instruction, that you may gain wisdom in the future (Proverbs 19:20).

Approximately 20 years after his initial surgery, my dad began experiencing severe headache symptoms again. It was determined that the original clamp used in surgery to stop the bleeding was now damaged and allowing blood to leak into his skull. Another surgery was planned to replace this clamp.

Karen and I went up to be with my family during the surgery. However, I did not visit my dad during his recovery time in the hospital. Even today, I cannot adequately express my total embarrassment and shame about this.

As I mentioned earlier, I was very close to my mom, and the relationship between my mother and father had deteriorated badly by this time. I now realize that sadly I held terribly misdirected anger toward my dad. Also, I began to realize, although I had not said it and did my best to repress it, I was still angry at God. I would think about all that I had missed by not being able to have a normal father during my teenage and college years and beyond. I was also angry because he was not able to be a grandfather to my children.

I was being extremely selfish, and now know that unfortunately it was my dad who missed out on so much. When I should have been loving and compassionate, I was selfish and punitive.

I desperately needed to find the road back to Christianity. In reality, I was so far off that road, the first thing I needed were directions to get back to it. I was lost, and the GPS was not getting a signal. The birth of my sons was a good place to make a new start.

Like any new father, I wanted to do the best I possibly could for my children. We started by having our boys baptized in the Catholic church. I valued the foundation of my Christian beliefs and wanted that for my children. So, I began taking them to Sunday school regularly. Initially we attended a Methodist Church that some of our friends in another community belonged to. Once the boys were of school age, though, we wanted to attend a church in the community where we lived. I attended services at several different churches, and we finally decided on a nearby Presbyterian Church. We attended Sunday school and church service there for several years until there was a major upheaval in the church that led to it becoming an independent church. We were not comfortable with all the chaos and change that occurred, so we began to look for a new church home.

Upon the recommendation of our son's third grade teacher, we began attending the Parkesburg Baptist Church. There was an immediate comfort level because we already knew a number of the people there. We attended Sunday school and worship service regularly. Our children were baptized there. They also participated in the youth group. We had found a church home.

For the first time in my life, I listened attentively during service particularly to the sermon. Part of this probably had to do with timing and the fact that I was finally ready to do this. I would also say that the presentation of the message by Pastor Jerry was done extremely well. He had a gift for selecting relevant topics and relating them to biblical scripture.

Prior to going to Parkesburg Baptist, I would attend church sporadically. I do remember feeling that it energized me and gave me a sense of focus and perspective, but soon after leaving, I would lapse into my everyday non-Christian habits. I now felt that for the first time in my life, I was at least trying to live my daily life in a Christian way. It was a start, but I had a long way to go.

As you may have noticed, our family has attended several different churches. We have been Catholic, Methodist, Presbyterian, and Baptist. What I have learned from this experience is that the differences are minimal, but the similarities are great. Although there may be small differences in doctrine and practice, they are all Christian churches, and all serve God.

It is interesting to think about the different people we cross paths with in our lives. Sometimes it is only a brief encounter, sometimes we have a relationship with them for just a short period of time, and then there are those who are in our lives for a lifetime. My experiences tell me it is not coincidence that we meet these individuals even when it is for just a short time period.

Pastor Jerry made a huge difference in my life. Being able to behave more as a Christian was a big step on my journey. I was treating people more kindly and respectfully. I was beginning to put others needs before mine. I began to find fulfillment in helping others. I would say I was only behaving like a Christian because I had not fully committed myself to God. I had not asked God to come into my life yet. I wanted that but still had a lot of questions.

Some of the most significant things that happened to help me move forward with my faith were through relationships with people I worked with at different times. The first was Beth. I had left Lincoln University and was working for an orthopedic and physical therapy practice in Lancaster, PA. We provided outreach services to local high schools and colleges. As our program expanded, we needed to hire an additional athletic trainer to work at Franklin and Marshall College. After collecting and reviewing resumes, we conducted several interviews and hired Beth. Beth was a Christian, and we had numerous discussions about faith during the time we worked together.

For Christmas in 1990, she gave me a Bible with a personalized note written inside the front cover. It is the Bible I am using now as I reference scripture for this book. Her message inside the book reads "John 14:6, 'I am the way and the truth and the life. No one comes to the Father except through me.'"

Because Beth had been kind enough to give me this gift, I decided I should at least read it. I started with Genesis and must admit my head started spinning when I got into all the ancestry. In Genesis, there is a lot of detail regarding family lineage. Then, in Exodus, there are lengthy descriptions of different Israeli tribe members. So, unfortunately, I stopped reading.

I am happy to report that I am now in the process of reading the Old Testament again. When I get to the parts that stopped me last time, I am now glossing over them a bit and not concerning myself with some of the detail. I think the important thing is to get the message, which I am doing. I don't think it is essential that I am able to remember all of Moses' ancestors. Another thing that is helpful is to have a good understanding of the New Testament and realize the amazing continuity between the Old and New Testament. It gives you a much better appreciation for the whole picture and God's plan for us.

When Beth gave me the Bible, I remember being appreciative and thinking that it was a nice gift. I wish I could tell her now that it was the most thoughtful gift anyone ever gave me because it helped transform my life. She was someone who was in my life for maybe three years but had as big an impact on me as anyone.

I don't think it is coincidence that God brings these people into our lives even if it is for a very short period of time. I remember for quite a while wondering why she chose John 14:6 for the inscription. I now realize that it is one of the most important verses in the entire Bible. It literally is an instruction from Jesus to gain salvation!

It has taken me an incredibly long time to accept Christianity. God has given me countless opportunities to believe; he has gently nudged me in the right direction. Because of my cynical nature and doubt, I am sure this is what I needed. There have been many times when I wish he would have been less subtle and simply gotten my attention by smacking me over the head with a two-by-four. Obviously, I am kidding. I know that this was what was necessary for me and part of his plan.

One Christmas Eve during this time period, I was looking through our local newspaper and was stunned when I came across the obituary of my first girlfriend, Carol. She had moved into the area where we lived and was a special education teacher in the Lancaster City School District. She had been killed when a driver in the opposite lane fell asleep, lost control of his car, and crossed the median strip. He hit her head on.

I attended Carol's service, and it proved to be quite a horribly surreal moment. It was difficult to accept that someone I had been so close to at one time was gone at a young age as the result of a senseless accident. I reflected on this tragedy quite a bit and tried to make sense of it as a Christian. I thought about Carol and her family. What would life be like for her husband and children as they tried to work through this tragedy? I thought a bit about my own mortality and wondered what my fate would be if it had been me that was killed.

When my children got a little older, I began to volunteer with Big Brothers and Big Sisters. I had been fortunate to have a great childhood and wanted to help someone else who was not quite as blessed as me. Also, it was a nice opportunity for my children to participate and learn to be there for someone who maybe needed a little help.

My "little brother" was named Johnny, and he was seven years old when we first met. Johnny's father had left the family, and it was he, his mom, and three sisters now. Unfortunately, there were drugs in the house and a number of less than desirable characters coming and going on a regular basis—not an ideal home environment for a young child.

Johnny was smart and fun to be with. I enjoyed our time to-gether. I openly shared my Christian views with him as well. It felt good to have made enough of a commitment to my faith that it now came naturally to include it in my everyday conversations. It felt good to share my faith. I enjoyed reaching out to someone as a Christian.

We saw each other on a regular basis all the way through his high school years. I still communicate with him on Facebook and see him occasionally. He is doing well, and I hope that I was able to be a positive influence for him.

I have been blessed to have several close friends with whom I have been able to openly discuss my faith. I would be remiss if I didn't thank Dan, John, Dick, and Dwight. Each of you have talked to me about your faith and have helped me. I am grateful to you for that and, most of all, appreciate your friendship.

I would like to tell you about several other friends who figured most prominently in helping me rediscover my faith. The first person that played a significant part in my getting back on the right road was my friend George.

I first met George while working for the orthopedic and phys-ical therapy practice. He introduced himself after one of the educa-tional programs we did. He is absolutely the best person I know. He is friendly to everyone, exceedingly kind and generous, and an exemplary Christian. I know he is not going to like this description because he is also quite humble.

I don't think it was coincidence that I eventually ended up di-recting the sports medicine program at the physical therapy center where he worked. I am confident God allowed my career to move in that direction. George and I would talk often about Christianity, and George would patiently answer my questions and help me along.

I had told him about my frustrations trying to read the Old Testament of the Bible. He took the time to write down a few different verses for me that connect the Old and New Testaments. After reading these passages, I had a much better understanding since I was able to look at the big picture of God's plan for man and the promises he has made and fulfilled. I will be forever grateful to my friend George. We only get to see each other once or twice a year. We do make sure we have at least one golf outing every summer, and we text back and forth during the year, mostly about sports. I will always be indebted to him and consider him one of my very best friends.

My next-door neighbor of over 30 years, Bill was diagnosed with multiple myeloma. He received a stem cell transplant, underwent treatment, and beat the odds by living for 12 years after his initial diagnosis. Bill was a good guy but had not been a devout Christian. To his credit, both he and his wife, Linda, were able to overcome their initial anger and bitterness about his disease and turn to God. They read the Bible regularly, participated in Bible studies, and attended church. I know Bill was at peace when he died, and I am confident that he is in heaven.

Watching Bill and Linda deal bravely with this crisis and seeing them embrace their faith made a lasting impression on me. I can thank them for the example they set for helping me move closer to finding my faith.

Another person who has been a key figure in my journey to whom I owe thanks is my friend Tim. Tim and I have been friends for about 30 years and have talked often over the years about our faith.

He has shared some Christian books that have proven to be really helpful. There is one that I found life changing though—*The Case for Faith* by Lee Strobel. If you have not read this book, you absolutely have to. It is an incredibly powerful book.

Mr. Strobel was an avowed atheist. His goal was to develop a framework of principles that supported his position as an atheist and then set out to prove it. He compiled a list of questions that most people would have to support their position that God does not exist. For example, an argument that could be used to deny his existence might be, how can God exist if there is so much suffering and pain in this world? He conducted extensive research through reading and doing interviews with biblical scholars, clergy, educators, and scientists. After compiling his research and writing his book, Mr. Strobel did a 180 degree turn and is now a devout Christian.

As I said earlier, I am a cynic by nature and tend to need proof to believe something. *The Case for Faith* is unquestionably the best book I have read in terms of providing that proof. The amount of research Mr. Strobel did is quite impressive. In his book, he thoroughly examines all the big questions about God's existence, and one by one presents very well-researched and objective answers. It is absolutely a must-read!

I am so thankful that God put these people in my life. Some were there for only a very short time and some are lifetime friends. Pastor Jerry, Beth, George, Tim, and Bill, and Linda all gave me something I wasn't going to find on my own. They gave me a piece of the map I needed to get me back on the road leading to faith. I firmly believe God puts these people in everyone's lives. We simply need to be aware that they are there for us and reach out to them. My Christian roots were beginning to grow again.

→11←

OBSTACLES AND OPPORTUNITIES

But grow in the grace and knowledge of our Lord and Savior Jesus Christ to Him be the glory, both now and to the day of eternity (2 Peter 3:18).

For a long time, I believed that our time on earth was a test to determine our worthiness for eternal life. I am not sure if that is something I was taught in Catholic school or I came up with it on my own. I thought we essentially had to earn heaven. I have since learned that nowhere does the Bible suggest that our entry into heaven is earned. And, really what could we possibly do to earn such a reward anyway? I now believe that while the way we live our life on earth is very important, our entry into heaven results simply from God's grace.

Our life is filled with challenges, and it is our responsibility as Christians to do the best we can to work through those difficult times. Surviving those challenges can help us grow spiritually. They are an opportunity for growth. "That which doesn't kill us, makes us stronger." I am sure you are familiar with that very famous and poignant quote by Freidrich Nietzsche.

I first heard this quote from a friend and thought he said Nitschke. This is another "old test" for you. Ray Nitschke was a middle linebacker for the Vince Lombardi era Green Bay Packers. My response to my friend was, "That is a pretty profound quote from an NFL linebacker!"

We are tested in a variety of ways throughout our lives, and as

Christians we can rely on our faith and find support from God to work through the challenging times. Because we have free will and often make wrong choices, we sometimes create our own obstacles. Regardless of the reason we face a challenge, it is important to ask God for help.

And after you have suffered a little while, the God of all grace, who has called you to his eternal glory in Christ, will himself restore, confirm, strengthen, and establish you (1 Peter: 5-10).

It is often when we are at our weakest and feel overwhelmed that we turn to God for help. This is one of the ways God reveals himself to us. We are human; therefore, we are flawed. When we struggle, we have an opportunity for personal growth. Do not be afraid or too proud to ask God for help!

Looking back, I can see challenges that were presented to me in which I failed miserably and more recently ones where I think I have done a better job. For example, if I look back at my father's brain aneurysm and the way in which it impacted our family, I know I could have done much better.

I was fourteen years old when this tragedy occurred. Maybe I was a bit too young to process everything and handle it a lot differently. However, at the time of my dad's second surgery, I was a young man and to have not visited him in the hospital is inexcusable. I don't believe that God singled out our family for this tragedy. God does not hurt people. My dad had a defective blood vessel that burst. Is it possible it is one of those things that just happened and at that time it wasn't something that could have been prevented?

Is it possible that Satan had a role in what happened? There was a time when I would not have really given that much thought. However, I am now convinced he plays a much larger role in our suffering than I would have believed. Finally, is it possible that

God did allow this to happen, but it was a way to bring us closer to him? That may be a possibility as well. Remember when you were a child and would get a vaccination? All you knew was that it hurt, and you couldn't understand why your parents would let this happen to you. Your parents knew that although there would be short-term pain, in the long run it would benefit you. Is it possible that it is the same way with God?

So, what could have been different? Our family could have handled the situation better. Instead of blaming God and withdrawing from the church community, we should have turned to God and the church for support. Instead, we blamed God and carried bitterness and anger with us that affected our behavior and relationships. I believe in a forgiving God, and I am certain that he has forgiven me. It has been harder to forgive myself. As I said, I believe God has been extremely patient with me and has gently coaxed me along the way. God has been there time and time again, providing opportunities for me. This has been most obvious to me when I look back at my career.

My first job out of college was at Lincoln University. After being there for about seven years or so, I began to get a little antsy and wanted an opportunity to grow professionally. I thoroughly enjoyed my time there and had an opportunity to gain a great deal of professional experience. The problem was that I felt like I was good at a lot of things but not good at any one thing. I wanted a chance to focus on sports medicine.

We have a friend Brenda who had injured her knee, and I evaluated it for her. I looked at her knee and thought there was a good possibility she had an anterior cruciate ligament (ACL) injury. This is the primary stabilizing ligament of the knee, and when this ligament is damaged, the knee is unstable even when someone is only doing activities of daily living. It was important that she have it checked quickly.

I called several orthopedic practices and finally found one

practice that would see her immediately. So, we headed off to their office to have Brenda's knee evaluated. While we were there, I talked briefly to one of the orthopedic surgeons about my interest in sports medicine and desire to begin a new career. He introduced me to the physical therapist in the adjacent office, and they then invited me to meet with them sometime to make a job proposal. I did that and worked for them for a year as a consultant before joining them full time.

I became director of the newly formed Lancaster Sports Medicine Foundation. At the time, I chalked it up mainly to my ability and charm and a little bit of luck. In time, I would see God's hand in the event.

I worked for six years as the sports medicine foundation director at which time my supervisor wanted to dramatically change my schedule. I really didn't want to make that change, so I began to make some phone calls. After one of the educational programs we had while I was with the sports medicine foundation, a family practice resident physician from Lancaster General Hospital named Bill Vollmar introduced himself. He had since become very involved providing sports medicine education and services for the hospital.

Bill was one of the people I called during my job search. The hospital was interested in expanding their sports medicine program, so I was fortunate enough to have them create a position for me as the program coordinator. I didn't assume that my obtaining this position was pure luck this time, but I didn't give God the credit he deserved either.

A bonus to this career move was that my good friend George worked at the facility where the sports medicine program was based. I would now have a chance to work with and see him regularly. Was it coincidence that I ended up there with George who would be so important in helping me find my Christian faith? At first, I thought so, but I now think God was directing me to where I needed to be.

I remained with Lancaster General Hospital for six years at which time there was a change in supervising vice presidents that unfortunately had a negative impact on the political climate at the hospital and our program. At the end of the fiscal year, our program was terminated. Fortunately, I was there six years and two months. Six years of continuous employment was required to be vested and receive a pension. God's hand again? I began to think it might be.

So, there I was almost 44 years old with no job, a wife, two fifteen-year-old sons, and an eleven-year-old daughter. Within a week after the announcement was made that our program was going to be ended, the Octorara Area School District Superintendent approached me and offered me a job. Talk about good fortune. He didn't even know I was soon to be unemployed!

The school district was going to make some changes, and a new position was being created. I would be the Director of School and Community Activities. The new position included being the athletic director, athletic trainer, and director of a newly formed regional recreation commission. Obviously, I was thrilled by the job offer and ended up accepting the position.

God had my attention now. Three different times he had provided me with a new job when either I was looking for a new one or in the last case, when I didn't even have one. Not only had he provided me with a job, but each position was exactly what I was looking for and located no further than ten to thirty minutes from my house.

We loved where we lived, had a lot of close friends, and didn't want to leave the area. God blessed us so we never had to. I knew it was more than a coincidence now.

I retired from the Octorara Area School District in 2011. I continued to provide athletic training services to the high school as an independent contractor until 2013. I now do some part-time work, providing consulting services for sports and recreational injury cases. I can thank God for providing this opportunity as well. My wife and I were attending a church function outside of Philadelphia, and we began talking to a woman named Bunny. I mentioned to her that I had been a high school athletic director and athletic trainer. She said, "Oh, my husband is a retired athletic director." She said he did some consulting work for attorneys as an expert for cases involving sports injuries but was trying to scale back his time. This is how I met Dr. Richard Borkowski, and he encouraged me to begin working as a sports safety consultant. He is a great person, and I am deeply indebted to him for helping me. But mostly I am thankful to God for providing this opportunity for me.

In addition to my career, there have been so many other times in my life where challenges presented themselves and God's grace enabled me to successfully work through them. Here is one of those times.

My mother's health was declining, and I was having a difficult time coping emotionally. My mom had smoked all her life. She did quit at some point when she was in her 60s, but by that point, the damage had been done. My mother was in the hospital with chronic obstructive pulmonary disease (COPD).

My family knew that my mother was dying, and we had resigned ourselves to this outcome. My mother had a long illness, and it was very hard to watch her gradually deteriorate. We did not want to prolong her suffering.

Personally, I was having a very difficult time struggling with whether my mom would go to heaven. She had blamed God and turned her back on him when my dad had his brain aneurysm. Up until the time she entered the hospital, she was still angry at God for what had happened to our family. I had tried to talk to her several times about her faith in the last few years of her life, but it wasn't something she was willing to discuss.

Aside from weddings and funerals, I don't think my mom ever

set foot in a church after my dad's brain aneurysm. I was praying that God would forgive her and provide me with some way of knowing that she was going to heaven. Then He answered my prayer.

A few weeks before her funeral, I heard the song "There You'll Be" by Faith Hill. It was the theme song for the movie "Pearl Harbor." It is a beautiful, heartfelt song about remembrance and gratitude. One particular verse in the song talks about how the other's love helped them to make it through, and that they owed them so much because of it. Some of the lyrics in the chorus state that they will always keep a part of the other near. About a week before her funeral, I was driving and heard the song again on the radio. I was unable to remember all the words exactly but thought that it might be an appropriate tribute for my mother's funeral service.

Within a week, I received a call from my brother John telling me that my mom was really struggling, and I needed to get to the hospital right away. So, I climbed into the car and got ready to make the drive to New Jersey. I turned on the radio and yes, "There You'll Be" was playing. I had a chance to listen to the words a bit more closely and realized they conveyed my feelings for my mom exactly.

It was a tear-filled trip to the hospital that night. I reflected on all the things my mom had done for me. Some were big and obvious, and some were small but no less significant. As I drove, I realized there were more of these memories than I could possibly count.

My mom passed away not long after I got to the hospital. It helped to know that I had found the perfect song for her service. God offered me assurance that my mom would be with him in heaven. The chorus of this song says that although they will miss the other, they will see them soar above the clouds. As I shared earlier, my father served in World War II and was stationed in the Pacific. This made the song even more appropriate for the service.

On the day of her funeral, we had to get up early to drive to New Jersey, so I set the alarm on my clock radio. The next morning, the alarm went off and yes that's right, "There You'll Be" began playing. Coincidence? I didn't think so. I smiled and thought, "Thank you, Lord, for giving me comfort and putting my mind at ease."

This was a challenging time as it is for any family in that situation, but at the same time it was a chance for spiritual growth. I felt that I had honored my mom appropriately as a Christian and God had provided me with assurance that my mom would be with him in heaven.

At my mom's funeral service, I thanked her for her unconditional love and for the countless number of things, both big and small, she did to demonstrate this love for me and all our family over the years. My father died from heart failure about ten years after my mother. I had been able to visit him regularly in the nursing home where he was living. I had a chance to apologize for how I had treated him. At the time I did this, I really don't think he was able to fully comprehend what I was saying, but it was something I needed to do. I should have done it much earlier. Fortunately, I don't have a lot of regrets in my life. But I have this, and it is a big one.

As we had done at my mom's service, each of us children gave a eulogy at my father's funeral. I thanked my dad for giving me the gift of appreciating God's beautiful creation. I think of my dad often when I am outside and enjoying nature. It is a great way for me to honor his memory.

→12←

KEEP ON KEEPIN' ON

If you wander off the road to the right or the left, you will hear his voice behind you saying, "Here is the road, follow it" (Isaiah 30:21).

I have often been critical and judgmental. When I was in my teens and twenties, I might actually verbalize what I was thinking. For a long time after that, they were simply embarrassing thoughts that would flash into my head.

I might be walking by someone in a store and would almost instantly develop some kind of opinion about them. In reality I knew nothing at all about them and had no right to form any opinion whatsoever. For example, I might see someone with long hair and tattoos so I would think they must be a drug addict. The fact is, even if this person were a drug addict, I had no right to judge them! I certainly have my share of shortcomings. And, if they were struggling with addiction, they deserved sympathy not scorn.

I have no idea how this horrible habit started and was extremely ashamed of it. I am embarrassed to admit and share this, but I think it is important for me to be completely transparent in this book. I really hated this part of me and have worked hard to change it. I do accept that as a human I am inherently flawed and will struggle. With God's help, I have been able to mostly eliminate these thoughts from my mind. Now, when I see a stranger, I try to substitute judgment with a positive thought when I first see them. I recognize that they are a child of God just as I am. Do I slip into old habits at times? Yes, I do. But it works most of the time. The point to be made is, I am trying. We are all a work in progress.

I think it is important to recognize that we have a sinful nature and that God understands and loves and forgives us anyway. My faith journey has been slow and has involved small steps, backward steps, and missteps. I continue to make mistakes, but I think I am learning. I know that I will not give up on this journey, and I encourage you to do the same. You are human and will make mistakes. Be patient and forgive yourself but be persistent. God forgives you, and you need to forgive yourself.

I have had a good marriage. Like any couple, we have certainly had our challenges and our ups and downs. While we were raising our children, I was often critical of Karen for being too strict with them. During this time, I would say our marriage was fair, and I accept much of the blame for this. I believe that children do much better with discipline and firm boundaries, but I just felt that Karen was being too strict. I knew she loved our children with all her heart and would do absolutely anything for them. She had proven that time and time again. I also knew they loved and respected her. However, for some reason I held onto this anger for a long, long time and couldn't let it go. I was denying her forgiveness.

It took way too many years, but I finally apologized, and our relationship has improved greatly. We have been married for over 40 years now, and we are still working on our marriage. Our goal is to keep working at it and have a great marriage. "Do not judge, and you will not be judged. Do not condemn, and you will not be condemned. Forgive, and you will be forgiven" (Luke 6:37). The Bible really does have all the instructions needed to lead a good life. They are certainly not easy to follow, but the effort is well worth the reward.

Marriage is a choice. Like every other area of our lives, it starts and ends with choice. We make a choice about how we want to treat our spouse and what we want our marriage to be like. When we exchange marriage vows, we make a commitment. At the time most of us do this, we are a bit blinded by romance and naturally a bit naïve.

A lifelong commitment is certainly not what we think it is at the time we exchange vows. Really, let's be honest, how could we possibly comprehend the meaning of a lifetime commitment when so many of us marry at a young age.

Marriage has moments of pure joy but more often the day-to-day reality is much less glamorous. Although it may start this way, it's not lying in bed cuddling every morning. It's not breakfasts in bed or a romantic candlelit meal. That meal is much more likely to be a convenience store sandwich eaten at 10 p.m. because you spent the evening running kids around to basketball practice and piano lessons. It's not a clean home and quiet evenings spent snuggling in front of the television. Sometimes it is those things, but more often it is someone who steals all the covers or snores like a chainsaw (me). Sometimes it's disagreements and angry words. Marriage is about dealing with empty paper towel rolls and full trash bags that didn't make it to the garage without finger pointing. It's sometimes about biting your tongue and not saying the hurtful words you would like to say. It's about still loving someone even though sometimes they really frustrate you or hurt your feelings.

It's about having someone love you at your worst—happy or sad, young or old. It's about helping each other with the hard work of life. It's laughing about the times you accidentally did something stupid (of which I have had more than my share). It's also having someone that will listen to your complaints about a terrible day and tell you everything is going to be okay anyway. It's coming home to the same person every day that you know loves and cares about you, in spite of and amazingly because of who you are. Living with the person you love is not perfect, and at times can be hard, but it is amazing, comforting, and one of the best things I have ever experienced.

We all choose our attitude and what kind of day we are going to have. We choose our attitude and decide how we will approach problems as well. I am sure you are familiar with Charles Swindoll's famous verse on attitude:

The longer I live, the more I realize the impact of attitude on life. Attitude, to me, is more important than facts. It is more important than the past, than education, than money, than circumstances, than failures, than successes, than what other people think or say or do. It is more important than appearance, giftedness or skill. It will make or break a company...a church...a home. The remarkable thing is we have a choice every day regarding the attitude we will embrace for that day. We cannot change our past...we cannot change the fact that people will act in a certain way. We cannot change the inevitable. The only thing we can do is play on the one string we have, and that is our attitude...I am convinced that life is 10% what happens to me and 90% how I react to it. And so, it is with you...we are in charge of our attitudes.

Now certainly, there are things that happen that make having a positive attitude challenging. But, with effort, we can control our attitude. Having faith in God and understanding that he loves and cares for us help us have a positive attitude.

I came across the following inspirational story (author unknown) about persistence that I believe is appropriate to our discussion:

A farmer's only donkey fell into an old abandoned well. This donkey was the farmer's companion and a huge help on the farm. The farmer tried every possible way he could think of to free his friend from this predicament but failed in every effort. In addition, there was a very good chance that the donkey was badly injured from his fall and even if he were rescued might not survive anyway. Finally, the farmer resigned himself to the fact that he would have to let his friend go and get a new donkey. He realized that the merciful thing to do would be to bury the donkey and let him rest in peace at the bottom of the well rather than letting him starve to death. With tears in their eyes, the farmer and his wife began shoveling dirt into the well to cover the donkey. Before long, the farmer and his wife noticed to their amazement that the donkey was rising higher and getting closer to them. He was shaking the dirt off and then standing atop each pile of dirt they threw in the well. Shovel after shovel, the donkey shook the dirt off and stood higher until finally he was able to step out of the well.

Be like that donkey. There will be hardship and you will have your share of dirt thrown on you. But don't give up, shake the dirt off and keep climbing!

The cold reality of life is there will be hardship and pain. In the end it all comes back to how we choose to process problems and our strategy for moving forward. I believe that having God in your life gives you comfort and provides perspective that makes having a positive attitude significantly easier.

☞13☜

FAITH, FAMILY, AND FORTITUDE

Family is not an important thing, it's everything. —
Michael J. Fox

One day as I was driving to get some lunch, my cellphone
rang. It was Karen, which wasn't unusual. I figured she wanted me
to pick something up at the store. When I answered, she asked,
"Where are you?" I replied, "On my way to get some lunch." She
asked, "Are you driving?" At this point, I was getting a little nervous. I told her I was, and she suggested I pull off the road somewhere. Now I was panicked. Oddly enough, I pulled off the road
and into a church parking lot.

Karen said, "Katie is pregnant." Anger hit me like a sledge-
hammer. I began screaming an assortment of expletives and
pounded away on the dashboard of my car. Our 18-year-old
daughter Katie was a second semester freshman at Washington
College in Maryland and was dating a boy we were not enamored
with, to say the least. We found him to be very irresponsible and
immature, an impression that never really changed.

I could not understand how my daughter could have been so
reckless. Although, as I thought about it later, I certainly had many
times through my high school and college life where I didn't use
good judgment.

This boyfriend could be quite charming at times and was also
very manipulative. Karen told me they wanted to come to our
house that night and talk to us. I said I was not ready to do that,

and we ended up meeting with them a couple of nights later. As it turned out, I still wasn't ready to talk to them. I know I did a lot of the talking and was still not able to control my emotions very well. I do recall yelling an expletive at them and telling them they didn't have a "clue," which of course they didn't. Not one of my better moments, and I was quite embarrassed by my outburst.

Once I calmed down and thought about it, I realized we had two choices. Either we could continue to be angry and risk losing our daughter, or we could provide support and do everything possible to help. Fortunately, we chose the latter.

In hindsight, if my daughter had never told us about the pregnancy and gotten an abortion, we wouldn't have known anything, and life would have gone on. I am so thankful that despite the circumstances at the time, this was never an option for Katie. However, her boyfriend did want her to consider this.

On Labor Day 2007, we got a call from emergency services informing us that Katie had been airlifted to the hospital. She had been in a serious car accident while she was driving back to college. She was struck on the driver's side of the car in a head-on crash. The entire front of the driver's side of the car was compressed into the cabin of the car. We rushed to the hospital to find her in intensive care in stable condition. Fortunately, aside from some lacerations that required stitches and some big bruises, Katie was going to be fine. The doctor told her that the baby probably saved her life. All of the cushioning in front of her acted like an additional airbag and protected her! Both Katie and the baby were going to be fine. We all thanked God for saving her and the baby.

Because Katie and her boyfriend were both young and students without the financial means to support a child, they made arrangements to have the baby adopted. My wife and I agonized over this choice. This was going to be our first grandchild! We talked a couple of times about having Karen stay home to watch the baby, but we were both working full time and really could not afford to lose one of our salaries. This was the harsh reality at the time and as we all know, life is full of them and the extremely tough decisions that follow.

At about 8:00 the morning of December 3, 2007 we got a call that our grandchild, Elizabeth Rebecca, had been born. I recall both Karen and I receiving this news with mixed emotions. We were thrilled by the news that Elizabeth had arrived and that both she and Katie were doing well. But we had to temper our enthusiasm because we knew she would not be a member of our family for very long.

Both Karen and I have loved being parents, but I am not sure either of us were prepared for the overwhelming love and immediate connection we felt when we held Elizabeth for the first time. Of course, this made the impending adoption even more difficult. So, we went home and prepared to go to the hospital the next day to pick up Katie and say goodbye to our granddaughter.

Karen and I talked again that night in bed just before we went to sleep. I can still hear Karen say, "We have to keep her." I remember turning over and saying, "I want to too, but we just can't afford it." I awoke the next morning dreading the trip to the hospital and our day ahead. I know I did not sleep well that night and I am quite sure Karen didn't either. I remember lying in bed thinking about Elizabeth and our decision to give her up for adoption. I finally closed my eyes and prayed to God, "Please help me, what should we do?" The answer came immediately, and I turned to Karen and said, "You're right, we have to keep her." After some tears and hugs, we called Katie and her boyfriend and told them if they wanted to keep Elizabeth, "We would find a way to make it work."

It scares me to this day when I think about how close we came to letting Elizabeth go. I am so grateful to Karen for wanting to keep her. If she had not brought the idea up, I am pretty sure that Elizabeth would have been adopted. God had changed my heart. I am so thankful that we made the right decision. We had made the decision with our hearts and took a leap of faith. We decided that Karen would take early retirement from teaching and stay home to babysit Elizabeth.

Katie and her boyfriend stayed with us for a while and then were able to afford an apartment. They married and attempted to provide a suitable home for Elizabeth, but as I mentioned earlier, her boyfriend was entirely too immature and irresponsible for this to work. He really was not able to manage his own life, let alone handle the added responsibility of a wife and child.

Sadly, we found out later he had been abusive to Katie as well. They separated and then divorced within a year of being married. Obviously, all of this was a tremendous emotional stress for Katie, and it has taken her a long time to resolve her feelings of anger and guilt. Fortunately, she turned toward God for help. His love and grace have helped all of us to move forward.

Of my siblings, I was closest to my sister, Joanne. When we were young kids, we would play house or dress up and play games together all of the time. She was Robin to my Batman. No, literally she was. We would watch that corny 1960s television series and were then inspired to play the characters. Our stuffed animals were the villains, "The Penguin," "The Joker" and "The Riddler." "Biff, Boff, Pow!" Needless to say, Batman and Robin were able to defeat their foes, justice prevailed, and all was good in Gotham City.

After having her first child, I am pretty sure Joanne, or Jo as I like to call her, suffered from postpartum depression. She was emotionally down and just couldn't seem to shake it. Unfortunately, she had always been a bit introverted and tried to manage the problem she was having by herself. In addition, her son was colicky, and her husband worked long hours on Wall Street.

She began to drink a glass of wine in the evening to help her relax, and soon the drinks became more frequent and the alcohol content stronger. She ended up getting divorced and losing her family. By 2013, she had remarried and was living outside of Philadelphia. Her new husband was verbally abusing her, drinking, and taking drugs. She was concerned for her safety, so she left him.

Jo had been in and out of different alcohol rehabilitation centers numerous times. As I am sure you know, there is often a typical pattern of sobriety and then relapse. This had been the case with my sister. I will say, of all the places she had been she has had the most success with the Salvation Army. She has been to some quite expensive, private centers, but she has had the most success there. The work program has helped keep her focused and active, and the Christian component of the program has been quite beneficial for her as well.

I asked Jo to come live with us temporarily. I was hoping that removing her from the environment she was in would give both she and her husband time and space to rest and recover. The plan was then to have them reunite and work on their relationship together at some point in the near future.

We scheduled regular counseling for her and found her a job. Like everyone in our family, she loves dogs, so we were thrilled when we were able to get her a job working at a dog grooming shop close by.

Things were going well, and she appeared to be content and making improvement. I remember smelling mouthwash on her breath one day and asked about it. She looked at me like I had two heads and said, "Everyone uses mouthwash." I replied that while there was some truth in that statement, not everyone was a recovering alcoholic, so I didn't think it was a good idea for her to be using it. There were several more times when I smelled mouthwash and confronted her, which were followed by the same incredulous look.

One night she didn't come home from work. Usually, she rode her bike back and forth to work, but it was late and getting dark. I was worried something had happened. I called the shop and asked the owner if she knew where Jo was. She said no, but after a brief pause said she did have one idea of where Jo might be. Karen and I met the shop owner at a local motel and found her in a room quite drunk and incoherent.

I took her to the hospital emergency room to be admitted for detoxification. Unfortunately, she never got the opportunity to reconcile with her husband. She had been in and out of rehabilitation programs, and her husband died during the time she was away.

I had hoped that we could help and make a difference for her. I was forced to realize that despite our best intentions and support, recovery is up to the alcoholic. I know she has had an extremely difficult time and I want to help her. I just finally realized that it is up to her.

She has now completed the program at the Salvation Army and is back in nearby Philadelphia. I have had several great visits with her recently and will continue to be a part of her life. Our discussions have centered on having faith in God, continuing to fight, and never giving up. I pray God will hold her close, and she will be able to finally find peace and sobriety. I will continue to support and love her, but I cannot allow myself to take responsibility for her recovery. I know my sister has had a difficult life. I have asked myself why all of this has happened to her. What I do know is that she is a Christian and is in a good place with her relationship with God. After all she has been through, above all else I am so glad she has that.

About two years after her divorce, Katie began dating a young man named Ryan. He was several years older than her, mature, and established in a career. He was kind and respectful and treated Katie and Elizabeth well. Karen and I liked him immediately. After dating for a few months, Katie informed us that she was pregnant. We were concerned because they hadn't been dating that long and didn't have an established relationship. I was upset but didn't freak out this time. I suppose part of this was because we had been through this before, but it probably had more to do with the fact that we liked Ryan and felt he could be a good father and husband.

We supported them and told them we would give them whatever help they needed, including babysitting. Our grandson Eomer (pronounced A-Oh-Mare) was born in April 2014. For those of you who have read "Lord of the Rings," you will recognize that name as being the nephew of the King of Rohan. Saying my daughter likes Lord of the Rings is a real understatement. She is fanatical! The name Eomer is of Gaelic origin and means "famous with horses." Katie has spent a great deal of her career working at equestrian centers training horses and providing lessons to riding clients. So, of course the name is meaningful to her. We tried to talk her into a different name, thinking it was so unique it may lead to teasing and bullying once Eomer was in school. But to be honest, I now love the name and love my daughter's strength of conviction (she would tell you I don't always love it!) for not wavering on the name selection.

My daughter is such an avid horse enthusiast that she and Ryan chose to get married in a barn. It was pretty cool. The ceremony area was toward the front of the barn. The barn was decorated with hanging flowers, ribbons, and bows. They had beautifully decorated tables with white linen tablecloths and fresh flowers. The best part about the wedding, though, was that I got to marry them! Pennsylvania law permits non-clergy to perform a wedding ceremony. When Katie first asked me, I was a bit shocked. It certainly wasn't something I had ever done or considered doing. However, the more I thought about it, the more I liked the idea. It was an honor for me to be asked and a privilege to marry them. How many times does the father of the bride get a chance to say exactly what is on his mind at a wedding? Well, I did!

In the fall of 2018, Ryan began having some difficulties with alcoholism, and he and Katie's home life became bad enough that

Katie and the kids came to live with us full time. Ryan moved in with his parents. Katie gave him the time and space to focus on the issues underlying his alcoholism. To his credit, Ryan did everything he needed to do. He began attending Alcoholics Anonymous and getting counseling immediately and has now moved back in with us.

He, Katie, and the kids have begun attending church regularly. Ryan and Katie go to Bible studies individually and as a couple. They participate in marriage counseling as well. I stated earlier that marriage is a choice. I am thankful that Ryan and Katie have chosen to participate in counseling to save their marriage.

Elizabeth sees a counselor as well. She has certainly experienced her share of upheaval in her young life, and counseling has proven helpful for her. I am so proud of Katie. These challenges have certainly been hard for her, but she has survived and is a stronger person now. She has found her strength and direction in God. I am also very proud to report that she is now taking online classes and is in the process of getting her degree in Christian Ministry.

God has led Katie to find a new job as well. Some of her friends from church work at "Sight and Sound Theatre" nearby. This theatre provides live Christian based performances and uses quite an assortment of animals in their productions. They told Katie about a position opening for an animal handler and trainer—an ideal job for my animal loving daughter! We were all very excited for her, and she loves her new job. I am so thankful to God that he has led Katie and Ryan on this path. They easily could have taken a different and more destructive road. I am optimistic for Katie and Ryan's future. I don't know how things will end up, but I do know they are both doing much better, and regardless of the outcome, will be stronger in the future no matter what life brings them.

Even during our darkest times, it is important to remember that God has a plan for us. Although the plan might not be clear to us; God uses all things for good. "For our light and momentary troubles are achieving for us an eternal glory that far outweighs them all" (2 Corinthians: 4:17-18).

Has it been easy for all of us? Of course not. Karen and I had been used to being by ourselves for some time, and Katie had lived on her own for quite a while. Obviously, the dynamics of the relationship in this new living arrangement required some readjustment. Yes, Katie is still our daughter, but now she is married with children. So Katie had to deal with the feelings of disappointment and failure from moving back home, and we had to adjust to the presence of four more people in the house. Simple things have now become big things. Since we had an empty nest, Karen and I had bought new furniture and installed new carpeting. Now we have two kids and a dog in the house. Of course, they don't really place the same value on those things as we do. Nor should they. Where things in the house had become pretty neat and clean, we now have clutter and mess. Zoey, the dog, seems just as comfortable doing her business inside as she does outside. She is lucky she is so dang cute!

Have there been times Karen and I wish we could have a more relaxing retirement? There certainly have been. Both Katie and Ryan have worked long hours for six days a week, so Karen and I are with the kids most of the time. And, as I stated earlier, Katie is also busy with coursework for her degree in Christian Ministry, so she often spends time in the evening working on this. Have we had disagreements with Katie and Ryan about different aspects of child-rearing? Of course, we have. I think that is only natural. We do what we think is right, but ultimately, we remind ourselves that they are the parents and should have the final say.

This is the situation we have been presented with, and we are all trying the best we can. It is not ideal, but it is necessary. Yes, it has been difficult at times, but our grandchildren have also given us many moments of absolute joy that we would not trade for anything. My approach to all of this goes way back to my early

Catholic education. We have been presented with a challenge, and we have a choice regarding how we will handle it. I choose God. I choose to believe that he has entrusted us to be very involved in Elizabeth and Eomer's lives, and it is a blessing for us to do so. We have been given an opportunity to help, guide, and teach them to live as Christians.

I was not happy about the circumstances whereby these children entered this world, but they are here; they are precious, and we will do everything we possibly can to love and support them. Katie and Ryan have needed some support and help, and we have been fortunate enough to be able to provide it. Again, we would have preferred none of this had happened, and it can be very demanding at times, but this is what we have chosen to do. We believe it is the right thing.

Nick Foles was named the most valuable player when the Philadelphia Eagles won their first Super Bowl. He has experienced the extreme highs and lows of a professional sports career. He proudly proclaims his Christian faith. Here is what he had to say about success and failure during his post-game press conference:

I think the big thing is don't be afraid to fail. In our society today—Instagram, Twitter—it's a highlight reel. It's all the good things. . . And then when you have a rough day or your life's not as good as that. Failure is a part of life. It's a part of building character and growing. Without failure, who would you be? I wouldn't be up here if I hadn't fallen thousands of times, made mistakes. We all are human; we all have weaknesses. Throughout this, being able to share that and be transparent is important. I know when I listen to people speak and they share their weaknesses, I'm listening because I can relate. I'm not perfect. I'm not Superman. I might be in the NFL, and we might have just won the Super Bowl, but, hey, we still have daily struggles.

I will have daily struggles. But that's where my faith comes in. That's where my family comes in. I think when you look at a struggle in your life, just know there's an opportunity to grow. That's just been the message. It's simple: if something's going on in your life and you're struggling, embrace it because you're growing.

Well said, Nick! Remember, we are the sum of all our experiences—the good and bad. Both good and bad experiences are important for our growth.

Mom (Marion) and Dad (John)

My first day of school— can you feel the excitement?

Jinny with Whiskers (who is apparently performing some kind of dental exam)

My sister Joanne and I "playing house"

Easter 1962 (left to right) Joanne, me, Jeff, Jinny, and John, and my father in back

My Nan with all of the grandkids– left to right back row:
Kevin, Terry, Jeff, Nan, Rob, John and Karen
front row: Joanne, Kathy and Me.

Buttermilk Falls

My dad with some future "Seeing Eye Guide Dogs"

Saint Joseph Church

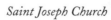

My high school graduation picture

Karen and I on our wedding day

At Jeremy and Melissa's wedding. Left to right: Matthew, me, Jeremy, Karen, and Katie

Katie with our grandkids: Eomer on left and Elizabeth on right

REASON TO BELIEVE

Introduction

Originally, we had planned to make this a two book set because as you will see, this book now changes direction quite a bit. However, the basic message is still the same. It is my sincere hope that by presenting my story as I did in Part One of this book and the information shared in Part Two that I am able to encourage you to seek God. If you are already a Christian, I hope you are able to develop an even closer relationship to him.

The second part of this book is a summary of the main reasons I believe in God and have chosen to be a Christian. I desperately want to help you in your journey of faith so much so that originally this part of the book was much too long. There was so much information that we were worried it might be a bit overwhelming. Instead of gently nudging and encouraging you by providing just the main evidence for the existence of God, I think I was kind of getting ready to hit you over the head with a big club! That is the very opposite of what I am trying to do, so the second part of this book is much more concise now.

In Part One of this book, I thought it was important for you to get to know me and learn my story. I am hoping that you were able to identify with some of the challenges I faced in my life. Although they may not be the same as some you have experienced, some of the themes were most likely similar. We all face obstacles. For me and my family, my father's brain aneurysm was a significant trauma. You may have dealt with something similar growing up or maybe very different, but the bottom line is that most of us have dealt with or will at some point have to deal with something traumatic. Even if your story is different, you still had to deal with overcoming a challenge. This is a common thread that binds all of us. We and our stories are much more alike than we are different.

I can't really tell you when my journey of faith began. I suppose realistically it began with my arrival on this earth. It really is a culmination of all I have seen and experienced in my life so far. And it is not over by any means. It will continue until the day I leave this earth. I tried to think about what were the most important things that helped me toss my cynical nature aside and carefully consider evidence for God's existence and my desire to want to become a Christian. What follows is exactly that. It is a summary of those things that I believe provide the most compelling evidence for God's existence and the reasons you should want to know him and have him in your life. I call Part Two of this book, *Reason to Believe*. First, I think you have to apply sound reasoning skills to evaluate and draw the proper conclusion from the information provided and also because this part of the book provides you with many reasons to believe.

❧14❧

THE MIRACLE OF GOD'S CREATION

How many are your works, LORD! In wisdom you made them all; the earth is full of your creatures. There is the sea, vast and spacious, teeming with creatures beyond number—living things both large and small (Psalm 104:24-25).

As a self-proclaimed cynic, I tend to analyze and scrutinize everything before I believe something. I want proof. I truly believe there is as much or more evidence to support the existence of God as there is anything we hold to be true. The remainder of this book looks at this evidence more closely. So, let's start with our physical world. I think it provides compelling proof for God as our Maker and Creator of all things.

"The more I study nature, the more I stand amazed at the work of the creator. Science brings men nearer to God." This is a quote from the famous French scientist Louis Pasteur.

I think any discussion of faith should include the beginning. What about creation? How did we get here? Why are we here? As we pass through this life, we can approach it in one of two ways: 1. We can be indifferent to the world around us, never fully appreciating it; or 2) We can look at it in wonder and be amazed. I choose to be amazed, and I will share some of my reasons why.

There are different schools of thought regarding the origin of our universe. I am sure you have heard of the Big Bang Theory, which is one of the most popular of these theories. It is an effort to explain what happened at the very beginning of our universe.

Discoveries in astronomy and physics have shown beyond a reasonable doubt that our universe did, in fact, have a beginning. Scientists explain that prior to that moment there was nothing; during and after that moment, there was something—our universe. Excuse my cynicism if I say, "Well, duh" here.

The Big Bang Theory is an effort to explain what happened during and after that moment. The basis of this theory is that a group of atoms came together at tremendous speeds and began the formation of planets, stars, etc. These scientists tell us that our universe sprang into existence around 13.7 billion years ago and is constantly expanding.

The Primordial Soup theory, another popular theory to explain the origin of life, goes something like this: Life on earth first bloomed around 3.7 billion years ago when chemical compounds in a primordial soup sprang to life. This soup, present in the prehistoric oceans, was rich in organic compounds and sparked life.

Although the Theory of Evolution is not a theory about the origin of life, Charles Darwin did propose the existence of a simple, single-celled organism as the common ancestor for all life. One species then changed into another and so on. This is called macroevolution. Darwin also proposed microevolution within species as a theory to explain changes within species over time. This theory can be observed when one looks at the same species living in different environmental conditions. For example, animals living in the cold, harsh conditions of the Arctic must adapt and certainly look different than the same animal from a more temperate climate. As a Christian, I believe that God, who created all life, skillfully provided a design whereby animals were able to achieve the changes necessary to adapt to a new environment.

A discussion of the Big Bang Theory, the Primordial Soup, and Evolution is incomplete without asking an even bigger question: What about God? Creation was a supernatural event. Do you see any problem with these theories? I think we can all agree that you don't get something from nothing. Who started the Big Bang? Where did the atoms come from?

How did the primordial soup spark to life? How did the single-celled organism from which renowned scientist Charles Darwin proposes all life began and evolved from come into existence? I do not consider myself the most handsome guy ever, but even I am offended by Darwin's notion that my direct ancestor was a fish. There is no argument to explain the origin of the universe or life that explains how it started. Was there a master architect behind this?

We know that this universe and life had a beginning, so who started it? There can only be one answer and that is God. Hence the popular term, "intelligent design." James Tour, a professor at Rice University's Department of Chemistry and Center for Nanoscale Science Technology, remarks,

> I stand in awe of God because of what he has done through his creation. Only a rookie who knows nothing about science would say science takes away from faith. If you really study science, it will bring you closer to God.

Life doesn't just happen. I think it is very possible that when these theories were proposed, an assumption was made that a single-cell organism was very simple and could just develop, almost on its own. We have since learned that the creation of just one single living molecule has proven to be impossible for scientists.

Harvard University Paleontologist George Gaylord Simpson stated that a single protein molecule is the most complicated substance known to mankind. Even the simplest combination of DNA and amino acids is incredibly complex. Emile Borel, a great French scientist and probability expert, states the probability of making a human cell by pure chance is 10,119,000 to 1. He also points out that a probability of 1050 to 1 means it would never happen. Yet there are those who would like us to believe that life developed by pure random chance. Nobel Prize winner Sir Francise Crick states, "The origin of life appears to be almost a miracle, so many are the conditions which would have to been satisfied to get it going"

Here is another problem. If you use science to explain what happened, the history of earth will always be changing. Science is dynamic and always evolving. As technology advances and our information base expands, what is true today may not be true tomorrow. History is constant and is the foundation for all other disciplines. We should probably let history tell us *what* happened, and science tell us *how* it happened.

We live on a planet that, to the best of our knowledge, is the only one that can support life or at least life as we know it. Our earth spins on an axis over a 24-hour period, turning toward and away from the sun to give us our night and day. It has done this forever and continues to do this day after day, month after month, and year after year.

Did you know that the earth is tilted on its axis at an angle of 23 degrees? That is a rather odd number, don't you think? Why not 15, 30 or 45 degrees? Well, a 23-degree angle ensures that the earth is turned slowly on all parts of its surface to optimize exposure to the sun. If there were no tilt, the poles would accumulate too much ice, and the center of the earth would be too hot to sustain life. Intelligent design again. Actually, more like brilliant design!

The earth travels 365 days in an orbit around the sun, giving us our calendar year and our seasons of winter, spring, summer, and fall. The changing seasons provide the opportunity for renewal and growth as well as rest and recovery. The earth has orbited the sun forever and does this year after year. The earth's relative and unchanging position to the sun allows the planet to produce tree and plant life, much of which provides food and other valuable resources for us. Although we have temperature extremes, in most areas, the climate is suitable to sustain life. Evaporation of large bodies of water and oceans into the sky results in rain and snowfall constantly replenishing our water supply. It is literally the largest recycling system in existence!

Our atmosphere consists of 20.93% oxygen. This life sustaining gas is required by every tissue of almost every living organism on our planet. We exhale much more carbon dioxide than we inhale. While we inhale oxygen and exhale carbon dioxide, the trees and plants help scrub our atmosphere clean by absorbing this carbon dioxide and giving off oxygen.

Besides oxygen, our atmosphere consists of 78% nitrogen, which is critical to all tree and plant life. In the atmosphere, nitrogen is inert, meaning it needs to combine chemically with something to become available. The 100,000 lightning bolts that strike the earth on a daily basis take care of that for us.

Is all this pure coincidence? It seems very unlikely to me. Dr. William Craig, a Research Professor of Philosophy at the Talbot School of Theology, says "Scientifically speaking, it's far more probable for a life-prohibiting universe to exist than a life-sustaining one." Life is balanced on a razor's edge. He cites Stephen Hawking's research which states, "That if the rate of the universe's expansion one second after the Big Bang had been smaller by even one part in a hundred thousand million, the universe would have collapsed into a fireball." This sounds like either an amazing coincidence or incredibly well-timed planning. To me it sounds like God.

All of the systems of the human body interact with one another constantly for our entire life. Certainly injury, illness, or disease can affect them, but for the most part, these systems function quite well. The average life expectancy for all people in developed countries regardless of nationality is around 80 years old. That is quite a length of time for any system to work. Let's look at just one of these systems:

The Cardiovascular System

First, your heart is controlled by the brain. A nerve impulse stimulates the heart muscle, and it contracts. It is unique because unlike other muscles in the body, when the heart receives a nerve stimulus, all the muscle fibers contract at the same time. This is necessary for the blood to be pumped effectively.

Of course, the brain also relies on the heart for a constant blood supply. Like every other organ of our body, it wouldn't be able to function effectively without it. Our body relies on different systems in a symbiotic relationship, working together and supporting each other.

When the heart contracts, blood is forced through it and then out into the body. Every tissue of the human body relies on a constant delivery of blood and oxygen. Starting in the left lower chamber of the heart, blood rich with oxygen is carried throughout the body. The oxygen is delivered to all parts of the body by the capillaries, a branch-like network throughout the tissues. The blood, now devoid of oxygen, is then returned to the upper right chamber of the heart. It is then pumped into the right lower chamber and then to the lungs where it picks up oxygen. After oxygen carrying blood leaves the lungs, it is delivered back to the upper left heart chamber and the whole process repeats again.

The valves between the chambers of the heart and where blood vessels attach to the lower chambers of the heart help to prevent any backflow of blood. When a doctor diagnoses a heart murmur, they are hearing backflow of blood from a defective valve. Our heart beats on average about 70 times per minute, 420 times per hour, 100,800 times per day, 705,600 times a week. Okay, I will stop now, I am sure you get my point.

How many heartbeats occur in your lifetime? Do you ever think about it? I wouldn't think so. Do you take it for granted? Well, of course, so do I. Does it make sense that this amazing and incredibly complex system could occur randomly with no planning?

100

I just gave you a simplistic overview of only one of the systems of the body. There are a total of twelve systems, all interacting with one another in perfect balance! Looks like God's work to me.

Do you want more evidence from nature about the existence of God? How about the miracle of birth? A single cell from a male and a single cell from a female join. These two cells eventually grow into over 37 trillion cells as an adult! To emphasize what an incredibly huge number this is, here it is in print: 37,000,000,000,000.

Each cell contains 23 chromosomes. When the cells join, there are now 23 paired chromosomes containing all the genetic information necessary to reproduce another living being. Different chromosomes are responsible for things like hair color, eye color, skin pigment, blood type, handedness, brain, heart, lungs, hands, legs, etc. Look at the overwhelming amount of information contained within two tiny cells that serve as instructions for development. Look at how incredibly complex this process is. Yes, sometimes there are birth defects, but most of the time an infant is healthy and perfectly formed. A beautiful, healthy, amazingly complex infant results from the joining of two cells.

Did you know an infant's heartbeat can be heard as early as 28 days! A brand new human being with a beating heart forms only 28 days after conception. Amazing! I believe it is easy to see the hand of God at work here. Detailed planning, care and love. The birth of a newborn baby is one of God's great masterpieces!

I found an excellent online video by Ray Comfort in which he does an outstanding job of making people question the source of their existence and their faith in God. It is entitled, "The Atheist Delusion." In the video, Mr. Comfort begins by confirming that the person he is talking to is indeed an atheist. He then asks them if they saw evidence that God exists, would they possibly change their minds. Every person he interviews says that they would. He then has people look at a book and asks them whether that book could have been produced by accident. Could all the numbered pages, colored pictures, and text fall from the sky and miraculously bind itself together in the proper order to form a book? Of course, they all answer no.

Mr. Comfort then talks to the people he is interviewing about DNA, our instruction book for life containing incredibly complex information that determines our physical make up. Everything we are and will be comes from these instructions in each living cell. We have 46 chapters (chromosomes) in our instruction book, and each chapter contains between 48-250 letters. That adds up to over 3 billion letters in our book! So, he reminds them that they said a physical book was incapable of making itself and asks them if our book representing a human being, which is infinitely more complex, could have been made by accident. As you can imagine, it presents quite a dilemma for the atheists he interviews. If they weren't created by accident, then how did they get here? Take a look at the video. It is extremely well done and quite thought provoking.

More evidence of God from nature can be seen with migration patterns. Many species of animals migrate relatively long distances, usually on a seasonal basis. All major animal groups migrate, including birds, mammals, fish, reptiles, and insects. The reason for migration may be climate, availability of food, the season of the year, or for mating reasons. Whatever the reason, it is an amazing phenomenon of nature.

A small bird called the Arctic tern makes a trip of around 44,000 miles from the North Pole to the South Pole each year. That means it will fly the equivalent of three round trips to the moon in its lifetime! How can it do that and not get lost? How does it survive that kind of trip? It sounds like a well-orchestrated and well-planned event. An equally impressive migration feat is performed by the monarch butterfly. This tiny insect that weighs only about .75 grams, not even a pound, flies from the United States to Mexico every year in a 3,000 mile one-way trip.

So, how do creatures even know how and when to migrate?

How does a tiny insect like a monarch butterfly that you can easily hold in your hand and most likely damage with a forceful blow of your breath endure such a long trip and survive adverse weather conditions? Is it simply a matter of coincidence? Most of these creatures are not capable of problem-solving. It seems to me it is part of a very intricate plan to sustain life.

It is now early March in Pennsylvania, a time when it is not uncommon for us to get major snowstorms. But today we are blessed to have a spectacular 70 degree, crystal clear blue sky, and gentle breeze day. I used this beautiful day to begin removing leaves from the flower beds. I am pretty sure I just heard a chorus of groans echoing throughout the country. It is not actually the rather mundane and repetitive task of clearing the leaves I enjoy. I love that after I remove them, I discover new emerging plant buds, a sure sign that spring has arrived. I enjoy winter, but by the end of February, I am getting antsy for warmth and spring color.

I eagerly search for this new plant growth and then praise God for his beautiful creation. So again, I will ask the question: Does the emergence of spring or any other season seem to be a random, uncontrolled occurrence? The seasonal changes we see in nature are not random. They occur within a predictable pattern year after year that suggests planning, organization, and control by someone or- chestrating the event. To me it sounds like God.

We had a mother robin build her nest between the support beam and bridge of the kids' playground structure in our backyard. She picked a great spot for a nest. It was well protected from people, predators, and the elements. We were able to lay down on the floor of the playhouse and watch her tending to three babies. We were watching one day, and my grandson asked me, "Papa, how does she know to make a nest for her babies?" My reply was, "Well, God told her that is what she needs to do." As we watched, the mother flew off, got some worms, and brought them back to the baby birds. My grandson asked, "Papa, how does she know where to get the worms?" I replied, "God has told her where she can find food." We watched as she came back to the nest and shared a meal with the baby birds. My grandson asked, "Well, how does she know that she has to feed her babies?" Again, my answer was, "That is what God has told her she needs to do."

I laughed when we had finally finished this little nature lesson. Afterward, I thought that although my answers were very simplistic, I am not sure even if I had spent countless hours researching his questions, I could have come up with better ones.

Think about how many things go on around us constantly that we don't take time to observe and we take for granted. Most seem pretty simple and insignificant. Yet the sum of all these small and seemingly meaningless events are critical to the survival of our world. This mother bird is not capable of problem-solving, but she does not need to be told her babies are hungry and need to be fed. She does not spend time laboring over the decision about where to build a nest or search to find the best place for food. She just does it. I know the scientific explanation for this innate intelligence is instinct. But, how did this pre-programmed intelligence and behavior get there to begin with? My short and simplistic answer is God!

Okay, I admit it, my curiosity got the best of me so I did a little research. It turns out that birds use both sight and hearing to locate worms. Have you ever found a worm under the ground by hearing or seeing it? No, me neither. So my answer is still God. He must have equipped them with pretty amazing vision and hearing.

As I mentioned earlier, I look at the world with amazement. I ask questions. The more questions I ask, the more I have unanswered and the more I accept God as the only answer.

The heavens are telling of the glory of God; And their expanse is declaring the work of His hands. Day to day pours forth speech, And night to night reveals knowledge (Psalm 19:1-4).

Look around you. Take time to consider and appreciate nature and all the wonderful and amazing things that are happening. Do these things happen with no plan? It seems unlikely. I see organization, planning, and an incredible balance to the universe and our life. Could all of the universe, the stars and planets including our incredible earth and all life on it have developed randomly from nothing, or is it possible that God, a divine being of infinite wisdom and love, created these things to insure harmony and balance to the natural world? What do you believe?

We engage, interact, experience, and learn from our world. As a result, we develop a conclusion and understanding of those experiences. For example, we know that air exists. We can't see it, taste it, or touch it. One way in which we see evidence of air is when we see the wind blowing an object like a flag. Our interaction with God is similar and relies on evidence. We cannot experience him in a way to which we are accustomed. We are not able to see and touch him the way we would another human being. We can't communicate with him the same way we would with another human being either. Does this mean he doesn't exist? My answer is a resounding no. We have ample evidence to believe in God.

In this chapter we talked about the creation and nature as evidence. In future chapters we will look at the powerful testimony of those who have had near-death experiences (NDEs). We will look at the Bible and archaeological finds as further evidence of God's existence. Just like the flag blowing in the wind showing us evidence of air, we can look at evidence that reveals God to us.

We need to meet God and develop a relationship with Him in a way that is unfamiliar to us. It is here we must humbly recognize our shortcomings as human beings. I completely understand how difficult it is to believe in something you cannot see, hear, or touch. I have been there for years and years. It has been a very long and slow process. Hence, the title of this book. I don't think there was a time when I would have denied the existence of God, but I wanted proof. One place we fail in our understanding is that we approach it from a human perspective. We try to understand and create proof of God through human understanding. At some point we must humbly accept our limitations as human beings. We are incapable of fully comprehending God. I am okay with admitting that there are some things that I cannot understand no matter how hard I try. The hard part is that at some point we simply need to take a leap of faith to accept and believe.

God is an all-knowing, all-powerful, eternal supreme Being. He does not need anything. The only reason we exist is because he chose to share his love with us. We are here on this earth and have been provided with everything we need to survive and thrive for only one reason—the love and grace of God. He is real, He is our Creator, and He is with us every day to guide and protect us. Everything I am, everything I have seen, read and experienced leads me to no other conclusion. "For we walk by faith, not by sight" (2 Corinthians 5:7).

⇥15⇤

DEATH: A NEW BEGINNING

He will wipe away every tear from their eyes, and death shall
be no more, neither shall there be mourning, nor crying, nor
pain anymore, for the former things have passed away
(Revelation 21:4).

What do you think happens to you when you die? Is that it? Is that the end? Newton's first law of thermodynamics tells us that matter or energy cannot be created or destroyed. If you heat water, it evaporates into a gas. Although you cannot see it, it is still there. So why would we be any different? Yes, our physical body will decay, but there is more to us than that. This chapter provides stories of the experiences of those who died but continued to exist before they were resuscitated and returned to their human form.

Suppose you wanted to check the accuracy of something. You could ask a trusted friend, but even if they have always proven reliable, it would still only be one person's opinion. How about if you asked 1000 people for their opinion on the matter? If all of them said the same thing or a significant majority did, you would certainly have to take that as pretty convincing proof, right? But what if more than 13 million people told you the same thing? I would think you would believe it since that is a pretty overwhelming number! Since the 1970s there have been over 13 million people who have had near-death experiences (NDE) in the United States alone.

According to John Burke, author of *Imagine Heaven*, the 13

million comes from an extrapolation of a Gallup Poll finding one out of twenty-five Americans has had an NDE. Imagine how large this number is when we consider the NDEs from other countries. Studies and surveys like the Gallup Poll done in the Netherlands and Germany found a very similar ratio or about four percent of the population. So, let's apply that ratio globally. The world population is currently about 7.8 billion people x .04 = 312 million globally. This means that over 300 million have had a near-death experience! Now of course this is not a hard number but only an estimate based on statistical surveys, however I think we can agree, it is a phenomenon experienced by an incredibly large number of people around the world.

NDEs are a relatively recent phenomenon because of significant advances in life-saving technology and procedures. The phrase, near-death experience, is a significant misnomer though. These people were not near death, they were indeed dead and then resuscitated.

The most amazing thing about NDEs is that a significant majority of people experience the same thing. The old, the young, the wealthy and poor, white, black, Hispanic, Christian and non-Christian, devout believers and atheists. Think about that for a minute! What are the chances that such a large diverse group like that would agree on anything? I think you would admit, not real likely. Yet, these people almost all experienced the same thing when their physical body died, and their soul departed. These people were all clinically dead, meaning their hearts had stopped beating and they had stopped breathing. The absence of those two things mean you cease to function, and you are dead.

I think that near-death experiences are far too often discounted, but in reality, they are legitimate proof of God's existence. Yes, I understand they rely on human testimony, and I realize there may be some non-altruistic motives for people to claim they had one. Someone certainly could be seeking attention or hoping for fame or fortune or both. But I would ask those of you who may be prone to doubt on this topic to keep an open mind. I am hoping you will consider the evidence, examine it completely and objectively before you arrive at a conclusion.

In his book *Imagine Heaven*, John Burke describes the near-death experiences of many, many individuals. The people he provides reports about were professionals, doctors, lawyers, and businessmen. He selected them because they were well off financially, so money or fame would not be a motivating factor for them to fabricate a story. Also, he provides accounts of very young children because as you probably know, they are typically quite candid and would have little motivation to lie. This is an excellent book and I highly recommend it. Mr. Burke does a great job presenting NDEs and relating them to the Bible.

A woman named Sheila had a severe allergic reaction during surgery causing her to die. Sheila shared this description of what happened next:

I found myself at ceiling level. I could see the EKG machine I was hooked to. The EKG was flat lined. The doctors and nurses were frantically trying to bring me back to life . . . I was completely free of any pain. . . In contrast to the chaos below, I felt a profound sense of peace. After I watched the nurse's awhile, a tunnel opened up. I was drawn to the tunnel and became aware of a bright light at the end of it. I felt peaceful. After I passed through the tunnel, I found myself in an area of beautiful, mystical light. In front of me were several of my beloved relatives who had previously died.

One example, right? Yes, but experienced and told millions and millions of times over!

Here is an example of another NDE, although a little bit different. *A Second Chance at Heaven* is a book by Tamara Laroux that describes her near-death experience and new life following her failed suicide attempt.

At fifteen, Tamara was well-liked and got along with most of the kids in the school she attended. However, she faced feelings of isolation and loneliness. Her parents had divorced when she was four, and although she lived with her mother, her stepmother openly rejected her. She says she did her best to hide her hurt feelings as she tried to be a good girl and not cause any trouble.

On the day of her suicide, Tamara cried out to Jesus as she pulled the trigger on the gun because she knew what she was doing was wrong. She hurtled through darkness and felt completely helpless. She arrived in what she describes as "the loneliest, most desolate, most frightening place I have ever encountered." She describes experiencing a sensation of being pelted by acid rain. She had an awareness that this is what she deserved and knew she had been separated from God. She cried out and realized there were other souls yelling out as well, begging for another chance. She describes there being complete transparency, so she was able to know the horrible things these other souls had done, and they knew all the wrong she had done as well.

She noticed a glowing horizon above and beyond her that appeared to be heaven. She then reports seeing a "mighty cloud" rushing toward her and a brilliant white light shaped hand reaching down to her, which she knew was God. She was filled with healing and forgiveness. She was lifted and floated over the landscape and observed colors shimmering with life unlike anything she had ever seen. She shares that, "Our mortal dreams simply cannot grasp the awe-inspiring reality of such eternal peace, joy, and beauty."

Despite desperately wanting to remain, she knew she was only passing through and would be returning to her present life. She awoke on the bathroom floor of her home, soaked in blood and struggling to breathe. She screamed out for her mother to call for an ambulance and survived.

Probably the most interesting thing about this book was the incredible challenge she experienced trying to share her story. Although if I think about her situation, I can appreciate it. Can you imagine a fifteen-year-old girl going through this experience? Adolescence can be a difficult time for anyone, even under the best of circumstances. You have all the physical changes that accompany puberty and the emotional ups and downs that occur. You are trying to figure out who you are and how you fit in this world and, as a result, your self-image is at an all-time low. You are stuck in that wonderful and awkward time between childhood and adulthood.

In addition to the normal challenges of being a teenager, you have just experienced a life-changing near death event. Look at the dilemma she faced! Imagine telling your friends that you died, had a brief glimpse of heaven, and now you're back. Think you might be ostracized a bit? The people who weren't that close to you or were casual friends would likely conclude that you are a bit crazy and completely avoid you. Even your close friends would have difficulty with this, and their relationship with you would certainly be changed—maybe not in a good way either. I am quite sure even Christian friends would have a difficult time processing your story. Is it possible some would even be jealous? Slowly but surely Tamara finds the strength to tell her story and eventually, through this book and her Christian ministry, finds her place and her calling.

A common theme among the stories of those who have NDEs is forgiveness and redemption. God gave Tamara an opportunity to change her life and have a relationship with him. God is kind and merciful. He knows us; he created us. He knows we are flawed and will make mistakes. He is forgiving and provides us with many, many opportunities to correct our errors. God wants us to acknowledge our mistakes and seek his love and guidance.

Dr. Jeffrey Long, a radiation oncologist was at dinner when a friend, Sheila (whom we met on page 109) shared her near-death experience with him. It made such an impression on him that since that time, Dr. Long has collected information from thousands of NDE survivors worldwide and his data reveal the following:

- 75% experience an "out of body experience" where their consciousness is separated from their body.
- 76% experience intense positive emotions
- 64% see a brilliant bright light
- 57.3% meet a mystical being and/or relatives or friends

Another really interesting piece of research deals with a study conducted in 2008 by Kenneth Ring. Mr. Ring interviewed twenty-one blind people (two-thirds of them had been blind since birth) about their near-death experiences. What is amazing is that they all describe leaving their body, hovering above, and "seeing" everything that was happening.

In her near-death experience, Vicki, who had been blind since birth, describes meeting Jesus and describes him as having shoulder length hair, a beard, and wearing a long robe. This description is incredibly consistent with others who claim to have met Jesus during their near-death experiences and is very consistent with how he is typically pictured and how most imagine him. Another young man named Brad, who was blind at birth, describes a beautiful bright light in heaven that seemed to emanate from everything. These descriptions and experiences are incredibly consistent with those of sighted people who have had NDEs. How remarkable is that!

Dr. Eben Alexander was a neurosurgeon, and in that capacity had first-hand experience with patients who had near-death experiences. He was a religious skeptic and to his own satisfaction was able to explain away these phenomena using science.

On November 10, 2008, Dr. Alexander was driven into a coma by a disease so deadly that only 1 in 10 million survive. Seven days later, he awakened with memories of a trip into another realm. His guide on this journey was someone he did not know. Later in the story when discussing this experience with his sister, he found out it was a deceased sister he had never known existed.

Dr. Alexander used all his scientific knowledge to find out whether his experience had been a dream. His research led him to conclude that when you are dead, all systems of the human body cease to function. There is no brain activity, hence there is no ability to dream. That left only one conclusion: that in death, we are conscious and exist despite our brains.

The evidence supporting Dr. Alexander's experience transformed him into a believer in God's unconditional love. Dr. Alexander was a well-respected neurosurgeon. Do you think it was difficult for him to move forward and share this experience and his newfound faith? Do you think he may have had concerns about what the hospital, his colleagues, and his patients would think? Do you think he may have had a concern that in sharing his story he might be labeled a quack, and it might affect his livelihood practicing medicine? Do you think maybe there was a reason God allowed Dr. Alexander to survive when the odds were so overwhelmingly against it? He thinks so and openly expresses that opinion and his newfound faith.

Howard Storm was a former art professor at Northern Kentucky University and considered himself an atheist. He was touring art museums in Italy with a group of students when he suffered a stomach ulcer that perforated his intestine. Here is what he says about his near-death experience where he visited hell. He felt himself in the hallway of the hospital and thought he was being approached by hospital staff.

As the grayness got darker and darker, they moved in closer and closer...Where are we going? How much further? . . . Shut up, Don't ask questions, You'll find out...At first it was kicking, pulling, hitting. And then that became biting and tearing with their fingernails and hands. Their cruelty was purely sadistic. I definitely lost one of my eyes, my ears were gone.

He states that on a scale of 1-10, the pain was a 10, and the emotional pain was worse than the physical pain. He says he felt a voice in his chest telling him repeatedly to *pray to God*, and he thought, *I don't believe in God*. He said in desperation he began to recite random words or phrases containing God from songs like "The Battle Hymn of the Republic," "Jesus Loves Me," and "God Bless America," and noticed the demonic creatures who were tormenting him withdrew. He cried out for Jesus to save him and then saw a bright speck of light floating toward him. A hand reached out of the light and lifted him up. He felt "encompassed by love that exceeded the sum total of all the love I had experienced in my life."

He began to realize that his life had been spent "building a monument to my ego." He eventually resigned his position as a professor and became a minister. That is probably the most extreme example of a wake-up call that I can imagine! Think about what a profound experience that must have been for him. An atheist underwent a complete transformation and became a minister.

Mr. Storm, like many people who experience an NDE, received a "life review," where they are shown a detailed picture of every moment of their life up until that point. The review focuses not on their accomplishments but on their relationships and interactions with others. The message is clear—those are what matter. God asks, how did you serve me? How did you love, and how were you loved?

There are several things that impress me when I read stories about near-death experiences. First, the conviction with which these individuals share their stories. There is a real passion and clarity as they present them. Reading or listening to the story of a near-death experience is captivating because it is incredibly sincere and hard to discount.

Second, consider how difficult it is for them to share the story, whether it is an awkward teenager concerned about losing her friends or a well-respected neurosurgeon afraid of losing his professional reputation, patients, and income. The decision to share their remarkable stories requires bravery. I believe that God provides them with strength to share their amazing stories and in doing so we are given one more piece of evidence to get to know him.

Another item to consider is the consistency in the testimonies. Almost all speak of being separated from their bodies and floating above it. They describe a sense of freedom and euphoria. They experience an indescribably bright light that draws them. Many are greeted by a familiar face to guide them on their journey. They are reunited with beloved family, friends, and relatives. Others speak of having a review of their life up until that time, and the consistent emphasis is not on personal achievements but on the love they have given and how much they are loved.

Some of those who have experienced an NDE have a difficult time going back and attending services at their church. Their experience is so filled with intense love and compassion that what their church can offer falls far short, particularly if their church is not teaching the overwhelming biblical love that God demonstrated through Jesus' experience on earth.

Those NDE survivors who saw heaven describe it as a transformative experience but feel incapable of fully describing its beauty. I read an article about a physician who successfully resuscitated a man who had been declared clinically dead. The man was so upset that he had been deprived of the glory of heaven and brought back to this miserable existence that he sued the doctor! It must be quite a place for him to do that.

Although there are fewer of them, the stories of NDE survivors who experienced hell are very consistent too. They describe a dark and desolate place devoid of light. They hear other souls crying out.

The final and perhaps most convincing argument to substantiate the validity of NDEs is that unknown life experiences are revealed. Dr. Eben Alexander found out after his NDE that his guide was a sister he never knew he had. Numerous blind people who experienced NDEs describe seeing, and they accurately describe things from the emergency room where it happened. The accounts of what these blind patients saw have been verified by emergency room staff who were present at the time.

There are approximately 13 million NDE survivors from the United States and most likely over 300 million worldwide. A really important question is where are those people who have died, been successfully resuscitated, and experienced something significantly different? I am confident that a fair number of Christians are among those who have had a near-death experience. Wouldn't you think at least one of them would have come forward and said they experienced something dissimilar if that were the case? I could not find a single story where someone reported experiencing something that was not similar to the accounts I have described. I find it quite amazing and admittedly comforting that I couldn't locate any counter evidence refuting these claims.

I do realize that we are considering the accuracy of human testimony, and some may not reliable. Certainly, there are some who were seeking publicity or hoping for fame or fortune. Also, I realize that not all the testimony is accurate according to the Bible. But just because it wasn't described with biblical accuracy does not mean it didn't happen. I think it is very probable that a non-Christian might describe an NDE that was not biblically accurate.

Another area that deserves a look is that there are numerous accounts of non-Christians including atheists having an NDE and because the experience was so profound, they became Christians. Where are the accounts of Christians denouncing their faith after an NDE? If a Christian had an NDE and it was dramatically different than what the Bible promises us, don't you think one of them would have told us? Don't you think they would consider abandoning their faith? I did not find these stories while doing my research on this topic.

Obviously, an NDE must be a very profound life-changing religious experience. When we consider the incredibly large number and diversity of the group, it is to be expected that some are not credible. So, again we look at the evidence. Look at the sheer volume of people sharing their NDE stories. Over 13 million people in the U.S. and most likely 300 million or more worldwide! That number alone demands our attention. To put that number in perspective, the entire US population is 327 million. That is a lot of people! I challenge even the harshest skeptic to poke holes in that many balloons.

Yes, some details of NDE experiences vary, but overall there is an amazing consistency to them—an incredibly diverse group of people all saying the same thing. Do you realize how unlikely that is? I simply cannot discount that many testimonies without considering them to be very compelling evidence of God's existence.

⇢16⇠

THE BIBLE AND OTHER
HISTORICAL EVIDENCE

BIBLE: Basic Instructions Before Leaving Earth

Although I wish I was clever enough to have thought of the above stated acronym, I'm not the author and can't claim credit for it. I really love it though and completely agree. Although the Bible is an historical account of Christianity it is so much more than just that. It really does contain instructions on how to live your life as a Christian on this Earth.

When we want to determine the truth about an event we did not witness, how do we go about it? We might ask some of our closest and trusted friends who were there. We might read about it or want to see physical evidence. Finally, we would probably want to see and experience it for ourselves. I am going to suggest to you that as you seek a relationship with God, you can do most of this, and in some respects, even more.

Let's start with the Bible. It is the official source of God's Word. It is an accurate historical account of God, creation, Jesus and his disciples, and Christianity. It is an important and practical guide on the teachings of Jesus, the way to live your life as a Christian and attain everlasting life in heaven. Now please tell me about another book that offers you that much. It's like reading a really great book and finding tucked in between the pages to your complete surprise, a winning Mega Millions lottery ticket.

Let's look back several hundred years ago at our own United States history. How do we know the Revolutionary War occurred? We can't ask anyone who was there. We can't go there ourselves. So, we rely on other evidence. We can read about it in historical texts and novels. We can look at documents from that time period. We have physical evidence consisting of homes, forts, and other buildings from that historical period. We can visit battlefields to experience the actual site where fighting took place. And there are museums housing furniture, household items, jewelry, tools, and weapons from that time period.

Okay, let's go back even further in history. We know that the Roman Empire existed. But how do we know? We can read about it since there are some ancient writings and manuscripts that have been preserved. Also, there are artifacts from that time period just like we have from the colonial period. There are building ruins, armor and weaponry, tools, and household items dating back to that time period. Obviously, since we are considering a civilization that dates its origin to 27 BC, there are not as many of these items, but they exist nonetheless. So, we have two significant historical events that we know existed. We weren't there ourselves, and we can't talk to anyone who was there, yet we know they existed. We accept that they existed on the basis of other physical evidence.

If we look at the Bible as an historical account of Christianity, we will see how it stands up under scrutiny for accuracy just as we look at other books to help us prove the existence of prior historical events and previous civilizations. The Bible was written by about forty different authors. These authors were separated significantly by time, about 1500 years. They were from different cultures and countries and wrote in different languages. Amazingly, their message about God and the birth, teachings, death, and resurrection of his son, Jesus Christ, are consistently the same.

The Bible is one of the oldest books in the world, and scholars agree it is the oldest book devoted to religion. The Guinness Book of World Records identifies it as being the bestselling book of all time with approximately 5 billion copies having been sold. To put that in perspective, the wildly popular Harry Potter series written by JK Rowling has only sold about 450 million copies. So, why is the Bible so popular? Because it provides answers to life's big questions. Most of us want direction. We want to know how we got here, why we are here, and what is our purpose. The Bible provides these answers.

Another reason to believe in the accuracy of the Bible is the painstaking detail with which it is written. For example, in Chronicles 9:22-25,

Altogether, those chosen to be gatekeepers at the threshold numbered 212. They were registered by genealogy in their villages. The gatekeepers had been assigned to their positions of trust by David and Solomon. They and their descendants were in charge of guarding the gates of the house of the Lord—the house called the tent. The gatekeepers were on the four sides: east, west, north and south. Their brothers in their villages had to come from time to time and share their duties for seven-day periods.

That is pretty specific information don't you think? Or how about this: in Revelation 21:9, after our world has been destroyed, one of God's angels reveals the new heaven and new earth to John. Here is his description, another very detailed and specific one.

It shone with the glory of God and it's brilliance was like that of a very precious jewel, like a jasper, clear as crystal. It had a great, high wall with twelve gates, and with twelve angels at the gates. On the gates were written the names of the twelve tribes of Israel. There were three gates on the east, three on the north, three on the south and three on the west. The wall of the

*city had twelve foundations, and on them were the names of the
twelve apostles of the lamb (Jesus).*

Attention to detail shows the biblical authors made a commitment to accurate reporting, which shows a commitment to truth.

The Bible has been analyzed and scrutinized more than any
other book in the history of civilization. The Bible consists of
sixty-six individual books compiled into one book. The Old
Testament was written from approximately 1400 BC to 400 BC.
The New Testament was written from 45 AD to 100 AD. Much of
The Old Testament is an historical account of God's chosen
people, the Israelites. It includes the writings of Moses who wrote
five of the books. His writings and the Ten Commandments were
immediately recognized as scripture. A good bit of information became law. In his teachings, Jesus regularly and consistently vali-
dates the Old Testament by referencing its prophets and their
messages.

For inclusion in the Bible, New Testament scripture had to be
written by one of Jesus' disciples, or someone very close to them.
The message had to be consistent with other biblical scripture, and
it had to have broad acceptance and use by all of the early
churches.

More support for the authenticity of the Bible that deserves
consideration is the fact that seven of Jesus's disciples were executed for their beliefs. They would not recant their Christian belief,
which is based on biblical scripture. It defies belief that these men
would die to perpetuate a lie.

In the Old Testament, look at the story of Noah and the Great
Flood. Noah was handpicked by God to preserve mankind and the
animal kingdom from the flood. This seems like a fantastical tale
until we consider that in addition to it being described in the Bible,
it is recorded in the history of numerous civilizations. India, Greece,
Mesopotamia (this was an area comprised mostly of Iraq but in-

cluded small parts of Iran, Syria and Turkey) and even some North American Indian tribes a continent away describe a great flood. The stories are all so similar that they must be given consideration.

The Bible is the only book in the world that has accurately predicted the future. The promise of a Savior, Jesus Christ, is foretold in the Bible over 300 times! In the Book of Samuel, God's promise to King David is,

> *When your days are over and you rest with your ancestors, I will raise up your offspring to succeed you, your own flesh and blood, and I will establish his kingdom. He is the one who will build a house for my Name, and I will establish the throne of his kingdom forever* (2 Samuel 7:12-13).

The second book of Samuel was written over 500 years before the birth of Christ! Here is an even older and more specific reference to the birth of Jesus Christ. Isaiah 9:6 says,

> *For to us a child is born, to us a son is given; and the government shall be upon his shoulder, and his name shall be called Wonderful Counselor, Mighty God, Everlasting Father, Prince of Peace.*

I don't know if a prophecy could be more specific than that one! The book of Isaiah was written between 600-700 BC.

Let's compare that prophecy to other religions. In the books of Buddha and Confucius there is not one example of predicted prophecy. In the Koran there is an example of a predicted prophesy where Muhammad says he will return to Mecca, which pales in comparison to Jesus Christ predicting his own resurrection from the dead! Unlike any other religion, the biblical prophecies of Christianity are typically detailed, accurate, and numerous regarding an event.

Dr. Norman Geisler, President of the Southern Evangelical Seminary has this to say regarding the authenticity of the Bible. Dr. Geisler states, "There have been thousands not hundreds of archaeological finds in the Middle East that support the picture presented in the biblical record." He mentions that ruins of all five cities mentioned in the Old Testament including Sodom and Gomorrah have been found. Solomon's Temple has been excavated. Nazareth, the small village where Jesus lived as a child, has been confirmed by archaeologists.

Look at the history of Babylon, considered perhaps to be the greatest of the ancient cities. It was impenetrable, consisting of 196 square miles protected by walls that were 187 feet thick at the base. It was a paradise consisting of magnificent architecture, gardens, and palaces. The civilization was unlike any another at the time, far advanced culturally and scientifically. Unfortunately, its residents became arrogant and abandoned their Christian beliefs. You most likely recall the Bible story involving the Tower of Babel. The Babylonians self-righteous behavior led them to build a tower designed to reach the heavens. It was destroyed by God. In 607 B.C., Babylonian armies destroyed Jerusalem, burned the temple, and took the survivors off to Babylon, where they were treated with cruelty. In Jeremiah 51:58,62, God says: "The broad walls of Babylon shall be utterly broken...it shall be desolate forever." This was written in the Old Testament, which had been completed more than 500 years before Christ arrived. In 400 A.D., Julian the Apostate arrived in Rome with the intent of destroying Christianity and re-establishing a pagan culture. While engaged in battle with the Persian army, he destroyed what was left of the walls of Babylon so that the Persians could not use them for protection. Not only was it destroyed as was prophesied, today it remains an uninhabitable desert as God had decreed.

Tombs and small, modest dwellings dating back to the first century AD have been unearthed. In 2012, the burial box of James, who was Jesus' brother, was found. The inscription on the box reads: "James, son of Joseph, brother of Jesus."

Renowned archaeologist Sir Walter Ramsey spent about twenty-five years working to disprove the Bible and the Book of Acts written by Luke. He was an atheist as were both of his parents. Finally, after having found hundreds of items that confirmed the authenticity of the Bible, he shocked everyone by announcing he had converted to Christianity.

The existence of Jesus and his disciples is verified by authors outside of the Bible as well. Flavius Josephus was a Jewish historian born in Jerusalem four years after Jesus was crucified. So, his writings about Jesus are very close in terms of time and place. Because of this, his writings provide an almost eyewitness account of this time period. Obviously, his writings are very old and his book(s) are not something you would come across frequently.

I had seen Flavius Josephus mentioned during my research for this book, but had never seen his book. That changed when we vacationed in Cape May, New Jersey, this past summer. After bringing our suitcases in from the car and unpacking, we explored around the house where we were staying. There were huge bookcases on either side of the fireplace in the living room. My daughter Katie and I started looking through the titles. "Dad, you won't believe this!" she exclaimed. In her hand she was holding a very old book entitled, "The Works of Flavius Josephus, The Learned and Authentic Jewish Historian." Coincidence? Yes, I suppose. But of all the houses we could have picked for our vacation, what is the likelihood that this rather old and obscure book would be in anyone's library, let alone a vacation home in Cape May?

Here is what Josephus says.

At this time there was a wise man called Jesus, and his conduct was good, and he was known to be virtuous. Many people among the Jews and the other nations became his disciples. Pilate condemned him to be crucified and to die. But those who had become his disciples did not abandon his discipleship. They reported that he had appeared to them three days after his crucifixion and that he was alive. Accordingly, he was perhaps the Messiah, concerning whom the prophets have reported wonders. And the tribe of the Christians, so named after him, has not disappeared to this day.

Very compelling evidence to support Christian accounts of Christ's death by crucifixion can be found in a letter written by Pontius Pilate himself to Tiberius Caesar.

And him Herod and Archelaus and Philip, Annas and Caiaphas, with all the people, delivered to me, making a great uproar against me that I should try him (Christ). I therefore ordered him crucified, having first scourged him, and having found against him no cause of evil accusations or deeds. And at the time he was crucified there was darkness over all the world, the sun being darkened at mid-day, and the stars appearing, but in them there appeared no lustre; and the moon; as if it turned into blood, failed in her light.

Let's consider, the story of Christ's resurrection. Dr. Craig, the research professor, whom we met earlier in chapter 14, presents several reasons why we can consider the resurrection an actual historical event: 1. After his crucifixion, Jesus was buried in his tomb by Joseph of Arimathea who was a member of the Sanhedrin that condemned Jesus. For this reason, it is unlikely that anyone would have made up his involvement. 2. Jesus' tomb was found empty by a group of women. Women's testimony was not considered reliable, and they weren't even allowed to testify in Jewish courts. To include their testimony indicates that the gospel authors were being faithful to accuracy. 3. There are numerous accounts of Jesus appearing after his resurrection on a variety of occasions and to numerous groups of people in different settings and locations.

Here is some more compelling evidence of biblical truth. It took Jesus' appearance after his resurrection for Paul to believe he was the Messiah and follow him. Paul was a Pharisee and very likely a member of the Sanhedrin Council. He was anti-Christian and intent on persecuting them. He was traveling to Damascus to arrest some Christians, when Jesus appeared to him after his resurrection. Acts 9:1 describes Paul's conversion from someone committed to destroying Christianity to perhaps its most ardent promoter.

> *As he neared Damascus on his journey, suddenly a light from Heaven flashed around him leaving him blind. He fell to the ground and heard a voice say to him, "Saul, Saul, why do you persecute me?" "Who are you Lord," Saul asked. "I am Jesus whom you are persecuting," he replied. "Now get up and go into the city, and you will be told what you must do."*

Paul was then led into Damascus by his traveling companions. Ananias, one of Jesus' disciples, restored his vision, and several days later, Paul began his Christian ministry. It is unlikely that God could have found a better candidate for conversion. What an incredible message about the redemptive power of faith!

Sometime later, Paul sent a letter to the church of the Corinthians detailing Christ's resurrection. This letter was a public document written so that it would be read aloud. His letter was essentially an invitation to those who doubted the resurrection to go and talk to eyewitnesses.

For what I received, I passed on to you as of first importance: that Christ died for our sins according to the scriptures, that he was buried, that he was raised on the third day according to the Scriptures, and that he appeared to Peter, and then the Twelve. After that, he appeared to more than five hundred of the brothers, at the same time, most of whom are still living, though some have died (1 Corinthians 15: 3-6).

Although in historical context, the apostles are considered brave heroes, the Bible story presents the eventual leaders of the early church as often petty and jealous. They were cowards who disowned and failed Jesus. Again, the Bible is portraying them accurately. If your book is fictional and some grandiose hoax, why not make them seem like superheroes? Instead, they are portrayed accurately with all their human frailties.

More support for the authenticity of the Bible that deserves consideration is the fact that seven of Jesus' disciples were executed for their beliefs. They would not denounce their Christian beliefs, which are based on biblical scripture. It defies belief that these men would die to perpetuate a lie.

There are many, many biblical references to heaven. In 2nd Chronicles 31:18 of the Old Testament, Jesus told his disciples: "In my Father's house are many rooms. If it were not so, would I have told you I go to prepare a place for you." In the New Testament, Matthew says: "Rejoice and be glad for your reward is great in Heaven" (Matthew 5:12). On the night before his crucifixion, Jesus told his close friends, "When everything is ready, I will come and get you, so that you will always be with me where I am" (John 14:1-3).

The testimony of a great number of people who have had near-death experiences describe the splendor of heaven and once again serve to substantiate the Bible's truth. Here is what some of those who had a near-death experience say in the book, *Imagine Heaven*.

One person recalls, "The colors and lights in heaven were simply sublime. They were the deepest, richest, most gloriously lush colors I had ever seen."

Another remembers the sky this way, "The most gorgeous sky ever seen here on earth cannot even come close to the atmosphere in heaven. It is bright because of the glory of our God . . .The atmosphere is something you experience not just see. It is golden, yellow, and white and had more colors moving throughout it . . . like the Aurora Borealis lights. The tree and flower adorned landscape is magnificent with a brilliant light that seems to permeate every living thing."

Some were fortunate enough to experience the heavenly city. One of the subjects interviewed by Mr. Burke in *Imagine Heaven*, says he saw "a crystal-clear stream winding its way across the landscape with trees on either bank." Another witnessed a "magnificent city, golden and gleaming among a myriad of resplendent colors." In Revelations, John notes,

> *Then the angel showed me the river of the water of life, as clear as crystal, flowing from the throne of God and of the lamb down the middle of the great street of the city* (Revelations 22:1).

Here we have the promise of heaven being foretold by Jesus himself to his disciples John and James. Then we have confirmation of that promise by those who had the privilege to glimpse heaven during a near-death experience. They confirm its existence and consistently describe its awe-inspiring beauty. You can read biblical accounts of heaven and have those accounts verified by those who have had a near-death experience.

We are confident that the Revolutionary War occurred and the Roman civilization existed because of the presence of documents, buildings, battle sites, and artifacts. In our quest to determine the accuracy of the Bible, we have essentially the same evidence and a little more. We have documents, buildings, and artifacts. In addition, we have the testimony of over 300 million people who have had near-death experiences, some of whom have seen angels, Jesus, and heaven itself. Why then do we have any doubts about the existence of God?

The following is a fantastic analogy you may be familiar with regarding the dilemma of human existence and our inability to comprehend God's plan for us. The original story was told by Henri J. W. Nouwen.

In a mother's womb were two babies. One asked the other: "Do you believe in life after delivery?"

The other replied, "Why, of course. There has to be something after delivery. Maybe we are here to prepare ourselves for what we will be later."

"Nonsense" said the first. "There is no life after delivery. What kind of life would that be?"

The second said, "I don't know, but there will be more light than here. Maybe we will walk with our legs and eat from our mouths. Maybe we will have other senses that we can't understand now."

The first replied, "That is absurd. Walking is impossible. And eating with our mouths? Ridiculous! The umbilical cord supplies nutrition and everything we need. But the umbilical cord is so short. Life after delivery is to be logically excluded."

The second insisted, "Well, I think there is something and maybe it's different than it is here. Maybe we won't need this physical cord anymore."

The first replied, "Nonsense. And moreover, if there is life, then why has no one ever come back from there? Delivery is the end of life, and in the after-delivery there is nothing but darkness and silence and oblivion. It takes us nowhere."

"Well, I don't know," said the second, "but certainly we will meet Mother and she will take care of us."

The first replied "Mother? You actually believe in Mother? That's laughable. If Mother exists, then where is She now?"

The second said, "She is all around us. We are surrounded by her. We are of Her. It is in Her that we live. Without Her this world would not and could not exist."

Said the first: "Well, I don't see Her, so it is only logical that She doesn't exist."

To which the second replied, "Sometimes, when you're in silence and you focus and listen, you can perceive Her presence, and you can hear Her loving voice, calling down from above."

That might be the best explanation of God I have ever come across. As I have said, I was a skeptic. I wanted proof, and I wanted it through human understanding. We are like these bewildered infants in the womb. I believe it serves us well to humbly recognize and admit our limitations as human beings and accept that since God is a divine being, we are incapable of fully understanding all there is to know about him.

The famous author, C.S. Lewis said, "You can't go back and change the beginning, but you can start where you are and change the ending." No matter where you are in life, no matter how bad things seem, and you are unable to see anything good in the future, remember God loves you and will always be there for you. Trust God and change the ending!

→17←

WHY I BELIEVE

"Surrender to what is, let go of what was, have faith in what will be" —*Sonia Ricott*

Everyone who searches earnestly will arrive at faith in their own time. Everyone's journey is different. Some have an epiphany, an "aha" moment. Some come to Jesus with their last dying breath. For others like me, the trip is long and slow. That is really the reason I wrote this book. If I have been able to make this journey, so can you! Certainly, I was provided with a good start as a Christian. I went to church regularly as a child with my family and attended Catholic School. I was part of a Christian community and raised in a loving Christian home environment.

As you have read, I drifted away from those roots, and the road back has been challenging with many twists and turns. As I write this book, I am sixty-four years old. Although I wish I would have become a believer sooner, that is not the path God chose for me. I am by no means done learning and growing spiritually. I will still have ups and downs and make my share of mistakes.

I have tried to be completely transparent and honest in this book so that you would get to know me better and have a good understanding and appreciation of the challenges I have experienced in my life. I was hoping that might help you better identify with me.

I was not a bad person, but I don't think I was a particularly good person either. I struggled and still do at times. I do realize that my struggles pale in comparison to what many people encounter and overcome on this earth. If these people and I have managed to find the way, so can you.

I am quite certain that God puts no timetable on us but gives us ample opportunity and patiently waits for us to come to him. Here is a great biblical illustration of this. It is also a good reminder that what God values may be different than what we as humans believe is important.

A landowner went out early in the morning to hire workers for his vineyard for the day. He agreed to pay them a denarius for the day and sent them into his vineyard. At around nine in the morning he went out again and saw others standing in the marketplace doing nothing. He told them, "You may go and work in my vineyard, and I will pay you whatever is right." So, they went. He went out again around noon and about three in the afternoon and did the same thing. Finally, he went out at five in the afternoon and found still others standing around. He asked them, "Why have you been standing here all day long doing nothing?" "Because no one has hired us," they answered. He said to them, "You may also go and work in my vineyard."

When evening came, the owner of the vineyard said to his foreman, "Call the workers and pay them their wages, beginning with the last ones hired and going on to the first." The workers who were hired at about five in the afternoon came and each received a denarius. So naturally when those who were hired first came, they expected to receive more. But each one of them also received a denarius. When they received it, they began to complain to the landowner. "These who were hired last worked only one hour," they said, "and you have made them equal to us who have borne the burden of the work and the heat of the day." But he answered one of them, "I am

132

not being unfair to you, friend. Didn't you agree to work for a denarius? Take your pay and go. If I want to give the one who was hired last the same as I gave you; don't I have the right to do what I want with my own money? Or are you envious because I am generous?" The moral of the story is "The last will be first, and the first will be last" (Matthew 20:1-16).

I am sure no matter where you are in your life, no matter what you have done in your past and how unlovable you may think you are, God still loves you. God doesn't care when you come to him. He just wants you to come.

Look at the life of Jesus Christ. He was an outsider. He was ostracized. His was indeed a street ministry. He surrounded himself with misfits and sinners. Mary Magdalene was considered by some theologians to be a prostitute. Paul, the man many consider the greatest disciple, persecuted Christians until his conversion to Christianity.

In his short life here on earth, Jesus offered everyone forgiveness, hope, and redemption. In his final days, he was betrayed by some of those closest to him, including Simon Peter. As he hung dying an excruciatingly painful death on the cross, instead of focusing on self-pity and pain, he pleaded with God to forgive his captors, "Forgive them Father, for they know not what they do" (Luke 23:34).

When Jesus' followers went to the tomb to anoint his body after he was removed from the cross and entombed, they were greeted by an angel who told them that he had risen. Jesus had the angel tell his followers that he had risen from the dead and was on his way to Galilee. In this message he specifically mentioned Simon Peter so that he would know Jesus had forgiven him. Simon Peter, when asked by Roman guards about Jesus, denied knowing him three times and was forgiven. Simon Peter whom Jesus loved and trusted, betrayed him. Yet Jesus forgave him.

There is nothing you have done and nothing you could do that is so bad that Jesus will not forgive you if you ask. Do not let your past define you. Make a decision to make a new start and move forward. If we look at everything that God has done, all he has told us and everything he has promised us, the prevailing theme in all of it is LOVE. The word "love" appears in *The New International Version of the Bible* five hundred fifty-five times. I think we can safely assume in order for the word to appear that often, it is purposely emphasized as a pretty important word.

God created an amazing and beautiful world for us to enjoy. Despite the bad things, it is still a pretty great place. Even more amazing is he has promised us that someday earth will be restored to a place of even more profound beauty, and all the evil and pain will be gone. Heaven will be the new earth. God has done all of this for one reason and one reason only—he loves us! Despite all our weaknesses and frailties, he loves us unconditionally. He loves us much better than we love ourselves and love others.

Is all this easy to believe? Of course not, but consider all the overwhelming evidence we have looked at. I really think there is as much or more evidence to support the existence of God as there is to believe any historical figure or event. To summarize, here are the reasons I believe in God:

Creation and Nature
William Provine of Cornell University states,

If Darwinism is true, then there are five inescapable implications: there's no evidence for God; there's no life after death; there's no absolute foundation for right and wrong; there's no ultimate meaning for life; and people don't really have free will."

Ouch, that is harsh! I am quite relieved that as we examined earlier, the good news is I think we can dispel Darwin's theories rather easily. There simply is no reasonable explanation for the creation of the universe and life except God. Every other argument falls short. The Big Bang, the Primordial Soup, and Evolution all have the same fundamental flaw. You cannot get something from nothing! Who put the initial molecule there? Who put the spark there? Who started it? Our world, the cosmos, and all life were a creation. You cannot have creation without a creator.

The world is so complex, yet there is amazing symmetry and harmony to it. Remember the earlier statement from Dr. William Craig, "It balances on a razor's edge." Look around you at the sun, moon, stars, planets, including our amazing earth. The air you breathe, the water, all living creatures, plant life, and trees. It was put here as part of an incredibly sophisticated plan. It was put here to nourish and sustain life. It was put here because God loves you.

To me it sounds like an intelligent design created by an intelligent designer, God. You either believe that or you think it was pure coincidence. Seriously, which makes more sense? As you look around, what do you see, randomness and chaos or organization and planning? I see God.

Historical Accounts and the Bible

Thousands of ancient artifacts have been found to verify the civilizations described in biblical times. Even the inscribed tomb of Jesus' brother James has been found. As I mentioned earlier, the Bible stands up under scrutiny for its accuracy. Unlike any other book, the Bible has accurately predicted future events. Writings by a variety of authors of different cultures, languages, geographical locations, and times are incredibly consistent.

The biblical truth is validated because of ancient manuscripts and archaeological evidence that have been found. People who have had near-death experiences relate first-hand accounts of seeing God, the kingdom of heaven, Jesus, and angels, all of which are described in the Bible. Think about all the books you have read. Is their historical accuracy that good?

Near-Death Experiences

I will admit that although I have read several books on near-death experiences and they all had an impact on me, I had no idea of the immense number of people who have had this incredible experience. I will say it again. If we look at the number on a worldwide basis it is most likely well over 300 million! If the number were 30,000 or even 300,000, that would be impressive. But 300 million people is an astounding number, and they mostly all describe essentially the same thing! Contemplate that extraordinary number! People of all ages, cultures, faiths, races, and occupations experienced this and provide a very consistent report about what they felt and saw. This is a relatively new phenomenon because of the advances we have made in life-saving technology and technique. As God has allowed our knowledge of science to expand, he has provided us with a phenomenal gift. We have yet one more way to get to know and believe in him.

⇢18⇠

MY PRAYER FOR YOU

> When life is rough pray, when life is great pray.
> —*Anonymous*

It is difficult to adequately express exactly what my faith means to me, but I will give it a try. I have decided it is a lot like a life preserver that I am always wearing. I often forget I have it on, and there are times I try to swim without it, but it is always there lifting me up. Now does this mean that I never sin? Of course not. Like everyone, I make mistakes and begin to sink, but I try to remember God is always there to keep me afloat.

I have not arrived here quickly or without effort. I still tend to be cynical and critical. I have questioned and examined everything I could find, and I have never felt such a sensation of contentment and inner peace as I have now.

Occasionally over the past several years of this journey and in particular at times while I have worked on this book, I have had an indescribable feeling of peace, calm, and joy wash over me. It is unlike anything I have ever experienced before. I wish I could bottle and keep it so I could open it and use it whenever I need it, which is often! I really hope with all my heart that you can find that same feeling.

I know God loves me and he loves you not because of anything we have done. It is God's love and grace that he freely offers all of us. God dwells inside every believer. He is a constant companion and protector in our walk of faith. God has always loved me just as he loves you. Although it sometimes feels that way, we are never alone. No matter how alone we feel and no matter how hopeless things may appear, God is there.

As I said, I was fortunate to have numerous friends help me along the way and was given many opportunities to grow in my faith. But I firmly believe these people and these opportunities are available to everyone. Open your heart and mind and be receptive to the gifts people offer you.

I challenge you to be bold and take that first step. If you haven't sought a relationship with God before, begin now. Maybe your situation was like mine and you were a believer, but for whatever reason, you turned away from God. It doesn't matter! God will welcome you back with open arms. Maybe you are a non-believer who is looking for some answers. God doesn't care how, why, or when you come to him, just start!

When all is said and done, I have improved my outlook, my relationship with God, my relationships on earth, and hopefully have improved my chance for an eternal life in heaven, or I have been duped. When I consider the overwhelming evidence to support the existence of God, I am confident it is not a hoax. I would rather choose to live my life believing in God and serving him, and find out I was right, than not believe in him and not serve him, and find out I was wrong.

Don't you at least owe it to yourself to investigate the possibility of God's existence and a relationship with him? What about the peace, calm, and perspective provided by welcoming God into your heart? How about eternal life with your family and friends in an idyllic setting that exceeds your imagination? Read the Bible, talk to Christian friends, pray and read books (I personally believe a great place to start is with *The Case for Faith*). If you haven't prayed before, simply have a silent conversation with God. Ask for his help. Ask him to come into your life.

I think another and more unusual way to arrive at faith is to start your journey from the other end of the belief spectrum. Start your journey as a non-believer. It is possible that may be where you are now. So, in order to maintain and validate this position, all you need to do is disprove Jesus' Resurrection from the dead. The Resurrection is fundamental to the Christian faith. This is the belief that God's Son, Jesus Christ, was born and died as a human being for our sins and was resurrected in fulfillment of biblical scripture. Jesus died so we may live in eternal glory in heaven. His death and resurrection are the basis of Christianity.

In order to prove Jesus did not rise from the dead, all you would need to do would be to locate his bodily remains. Therein lies the problem. When Jesus' followers went to the tomb, the body was gone. There are conspiracy theorists that claim the Roman soldiers took it. The problem with that thinking is that if the Roman hierarchy wanted to squelch the Christian movement, and they absolutely did, all it would require would be to find the body. It was in their best interests to produce the body. It really makes no sense that they would steal and hide it.

There are also some who maintain that the disciples stole the body in order to maintain the illusion that he had risen and was now a spiritual being. This too is extremely unlikely. His disciples were frightened for their lives and in some cases were tortured and killed. All they would have to do would be to produce the body, and they would have lived in peace without danger or fear. It seems likely that at least one of Jesus' followers would have confessed to the location of the body under threat. I sincerely doubt they all would have suffered torture and death as they did just to continue a hoax.

Finally, there is a theory that his disciples were hallucinating when they saw the risen Jesus. The problem with that belief is that Jesus appeared to hundreds of people over numerous days in a variety of locations. It is unlikely that they all experienced a hallucination.

In conclusion we have the Old Testament Bible foretelling of Jesus' birth and resurrection. We have multiple books in the New Testament Bible written by numerous authors telling of his death and resurrection. And we know that the body of Jesus Christ was never found, which would have put the Christian movement to an end. I think it is important to understand just how critical this fact is and continues to be. I think we can assume that every effort and resource has been committed to this effort. I am confident that archaeologists have left no stone unturned in their search for the body.

There are countless accounts of atheists converting to Christianity, and I have mentioned some in this book. Here is another one. The late Lionel Luckhoo who is recognized in *The Guinness Book of World Records* for his unprecedented 245 consecutive defense murder trial acquittals was an atheist. Obviously, this man was very thorough in his research and investigation skills and an outstanding attorney. Someone challenged him to look at the evidence of Jesus Christ's Resurrection in the same manner he did as an attorney trying a case and then determine if he was still an atheist. At the conclusion of his research, Mr. Luckhoo wrote this,

> *I have spent more than 42 years as a defense trial lawyer appearing in many parts of the world and am still in active practice. I have been fortunate to secure a number of successes in jury trials and I say unequivocally the evidence for the Resurrection of Jesus Christ is so overwhelming that it compels acceptance by proof which leaves absolutely no room for doubt.*

Needless to say, Mr. Luckhoo became a devout believer and advocate for Christianity.

For me, the major final stumbling block to my becoming a Christian was to humbly admit that as a flawed human being I was incapable of knowing everything about God. The limit of my human understanding prevents me from knowing everything about a divine supreme being. And I am okay with that.

Once I had considered all the evidence to support God's existence, I still needed to take a leap of faith. Is God and everything about him fantastic and difficult to comprehend? Yes, absolutely! And I believe that is part of God's design.

What is more difficult to believe? That everything you see around us—all human life, all creatures, tree and plant life and the creation, the order and balance of our world and the cosmos—happened by random chance and continues uncontrolled, or there is planning and organization. I think it requires a greater imagination to believe the former. If you believe there is planning and organization to this life, doesn't that also demonstrate the care and love of a creator? There is no other reasonable answer.

My daughter, Katie, shared something with me that she encountered at work which we both found interesting. Apparently, a co-worker told Katie that her grandmother was dying. Katie offered her sympathy and said she would pray for her. The girl replied, "We would like to believe she is going to a better place, but we are too logical to believe that." We were both a bit surprised by this statement. I think "logical" implies that you have thoroughly examined the available information and arrived at a conclusion through sound reasoning. I would argue that if you carefully examine the overwhelming volume of information to support God's existence and all he has promised; it is illogical to not believe!

We are being offered an incredible opportunity—to live forever with our beloved family, relatives and friends in God's presence. I believe that should require some effort and challenge. But it will be well worth it. Our spirituality and faith are strengthened through hardship.

I am not embarrassed to admit that I do have a little doubt about some things, which is only natural. As human beings we are prone to doubt. And if you think about it, how many things in this world can we believe with absolute certainty. But I think that is okay. Remember, I am a real skeptic by nature. However, I personally believe it is almost impossible to have true faith without some doubt. Consider this statement from Gary Parker in his book, *The Gift of Doubt*:

> If faith never encounters doubt, if truth never struggles if good never battles with evil, how can faith know its own power? In my own pilgrimage, if I have to choose between a faith that has stared doubt in the eye and made it blink, or a naïve faith that has never known the firing line of doubt, I will choose the former every time.

I believe my faith has been tested, withstood hardship, and survived. I believe in God!

Let me ask you something. What is your identity? How do you define yourself? Is it your job? Our jobs certainly require a significant amount of our time and effort. There is also a tremendous amount of time and money spent educating ourselves in preparation for our jobs and continuing to perform them well. It is only natural that they would play an important part in our lives. For many of us our jobs provide gratification and self-worth.

Maybe your identity is defined through your role as a parent. Perhaps your wealth or new car or house is what make you happy. The problem is, none of those things last. I am not saying they will not provide you happiness. The problem is they provide only short-term satisfaction and will not give you lasting gratification and peace.

I have loved being a parent, but children can struggle badly and fail. If my children fail, am I a bad parent? Is my identity destroyed? What about our wealth and possessions? Businesses fail. You can lose your job in the blink of an eye. At some point you will retire or be incapable of performing your job skills at the level you once did. What then? Is your identity destroyed and happiness gone?

The problem with defining who we are through wealth is getting trapped in the never-ending cycle of greed and need for more that comes with it. The minute you drive that new car off the lot, it becomes a used vehicle, and the next model year will be here before you know it. Chances are there will always be a bigger, nicer house than yours.

I am sure you have heard it said that "You can't take it with you," meaning you are not taking any material thing from this world when you die. And for the most part, this is true. That beautiful house and shiny new car won't accompany us to heaven. But we do take something with us, and it is really the only thing that matters in this world—other people will go with us. Our beloved family members and friends will be in heaven with us. They are what matters. Our relationships with them last forever.

We can enjoy worldly things, but we can't let them define who we are. The danger when making any of these things into the ultimate thing is you are letting them replace God. We establish our sense of self by making something other than God the purpose for our life. So, the basis for our identity can collapse at any time. Sin can be defined by doing bad things, but it is also when we put things in place of God. Make God the reason for your self-worth, and you will never be disappointed. "If you live for the next world, you get this one in the deal; but if you live only for this world, you lose them both" (C.S. Lewis).

Earlier I described a horrible habit I had developed of judging people upon first impression. I now realize how this started. I had always believed that we earn our way to heaven, and our life on earth is a testing ground. As a Christian I tried to do good things and treat people well. This was an important part of my identity. Unfortunately, I think what happened is that in doing these things, I began to be prideful and self-righteous. There is a very fine line between being proud and becoming prideful. As I began to keep score of the good things I had done, I became more aware of those who did not measure up to that standard. So, I became judgmental.

I am reminded of an old song entitled "Put Your Hand in the Hand" written by Gene MacLellan and sung by Anne Murray. Part of the lyrics provide a good lesson about not judging others when it says if you take a look at yourself you will see others differently when you trust the man from Galilee.

As I have said throughout this book, in my journey I have often taken one step forward and one and sometimes two steps backward. Like a turtle, sometimes I have retreated into my shell, and I suppose at times I have been flipped over helplessly on my shell. But eventually I decided to keep going. It is a process. I now know that I don't earn heaven. Let's face it, there isn't anything I could do that would impress God so much that I would gain entrance into heaven. And he doesn't ask us to do that. It is only through God's grace that I have a chance to get there. There is nowhere in the Bible that says we must earn our way there. Don't get me wrong, it is important to follow the biblical lessons of Jesus Christ's life and obey the commandments given to us by God. We should do so with humility and appreciation, knowing that we will often fail along the way. And that is okay; God made us and understands us much better than we understand ourselves.

I was provided with a good start as a Christian. I was raised in a loving family with whom I attended church regularly. I lived in and had the support of a Christian community. I was fortunate enough to have a fantastic fourth through eighth grade Catholic school experience. I turned away from my faith as the result of anger and bitterness about my father's brain aneurysm and resulting disability.

Fortunately, I was blessed to have people in my life who cared enough to share their faith and help me find mine again. God blessed me by providing numerous opportunities for me to draw closer to him. I love this quote from Bob Goff in his book, *Everybody Always*. "God isn't always leading us to the safest route forward but to the one where we'll grow the most." I am grateful to be where I am right now. It is an ongoing process, though. I am human and therefore imperfect. I accept this and know that I am prone to mistakes and failure. God understands this. All he asks is for me to recognize my shortcomings and humbly seek his forgiveness.

I am grateful that he sent his Son, Jesus Christ, to live among us and teach us how to live our lives as Christians. I am also grateful that he died for my sins and was resurrected into heaven so that I may live and through his grace hopefully become part of his kingdom in heaven someday.

Try something for me. Think about one minute of time. Not hard to do right? It is a tangible amount of time you have experienced many times before. Okay, now think about one hour of time. Again, it is easily perceived. That amount of time is familiar and you can easily do it. Now, think about something you plan to do next week, a month, or even a year from now. Still no problem, right?

Okay, now try this for me. You might need to put the book down so you can really concentrate. Think as far as you can into the future. Think about holding your children, grandchildren, and great-grandchildren. Now think about the end of your life here on earth. Then think beyond that. Try to think about eternity. Close your eyes and really focus. Come on, go ahead. Really concentrate and think about forever. It is inconceivable, right? I know when I attempt to do this it is overwhelming and can be even a little bit frightening. Now imagine living forever in a peaceful, blissful paradise with God and beloved family and friends. I think it is a lot more appealing than the less desirable alternative, which is hell.

Take a chance on faith. I wrote this book because I wanted to share my faith. Faith gives us the ability to" have confidence in what we hope for and certainty about what we cannot see" (Hebrews, 11:1). Have faith!

By writing this book, I was hoping that I might be able to gently nudge some of you to seek God and begin your journey. I have tried to avoid being preachy, and I apologize if there have been parts of this book where I failed to do that. I am hoping by providing encouragement and information that, at the very least, I have sparked your curiosity.

This is a religious book. I have had a lot to say about God as well. I think sometimes the words religion and God can be intimidating to some people. But don't we all have a personal philosophy and belief system that is religious? Religion is nothing more than a set of beliefs about life's big questions. Who are we, how did we get here, and why are we here? What is life about? And what should we be doing with our time?

So, I present a challenge to you. Assess your relationship with God. Is it what you would like it to be? If not, be brave. Be bold. Take the next step. You don't need to take all the steps, just the next one. Do a little homework so you can make an objective and informed decision. Talk to some Christian friends. Talk to a minister. Read the Bible. Read some of the books I have recommended. Is God real? Is the Bible an accurate historical account of Christianity? Can you really develop a relationship with God? What does being a Christian mean and how can it impact your life? Find the answers. It is certainly worth the effort and will be the most important time you will spend on anything in your life.

When I retired, I prayed and asked God about how he would like me to share my faith. Eventually, I ended up writing this book. My goal in writing this book and my most sincere hope is that I might help someone who reads this to begin their faith journey or help strengthen their faith.

I must admit, although I didn't expect it, writing this book has been a fantastic experience for me. I didn't anticipate how therapeutic it would be to do this even though it was difficult to write at some points. I was forced to admit many shortcomings and failures. I relived a happy childhood, including my Catholic school years. I was forced to remember painful times, particularly when my dad had his brain aneurysm. I got to look back and realize the obstacles and opportunities that God presented for me to grow in faith. Also, I got to fondly recall a lot of people who were and still are there for me and helped me with my faith.

Writing this book has been evidence enough of God's presence in my life. I have never particularly enjoyed writing or reading. I always considered them important and necessary but a bit of a chore. When asked by one of his elementary teachers who read to him at home, my son Matthew responded by saying, "My mom does." The teacher then asked, "What about your dad?" Matthew said, "No, he can't read." My son thought I was illiterate!

With God's grace, I think those seeds of Christianity planted way back when I was a young child, despite being ignored and not watered consistently, have somehow survived and grown.

When I consider all of my personal experiences where God has revealed himself to me, the magnificence of nature, the inspirational testimony of those who have had near-death experiences, the historical accuracy of the Bible and the number of meaningful archaeological finds supporting the Bible story, I am confident placing my faith in God. Writing this book has reinforced and strengthened my faith. If that is the only benefit of writing this book, it will have been well worth it. But if I can encourage one or more of you who are reading this to seek God, then I can consider it a real success!

When I told my godson, Brian, about the book being published, he was quite excited for me as I had hoped he would be. He also said that no matter what happens, I should consider myself successful. I said thanks and asked him what he meant by that and he replied, "Well, you will either sell books or you won't."

I said, "Okay, and if I don't manage to sell any books how does that make me successful?"

He said, "Because then, every aspiring author who was afraid to try to get a book published will see how bad your book was and will think, 'If he got published, so can I.' In that way, you will be responsible for creating a whole new generation of authors!"

"Thanks, Brian, I love you!"

So, no matter the outcome, writing this book was a great experience. I hope you enjoyed it.

God bless you.

Resources

The Holy Bible, New International Version. Holman Bible Publishers. Nashville, TN, 1986.

Everybody Always, Bob Goff. Thomas Nelson Books, 2018.

The Case for Faith, Lee Strobel. Zondervan, 2000

90 Minutes in Heaven, Don Piper with Cecil Murphey. Revell Books, 2004.

Heaven, Randy Alcorn. Tyndale House, 2004.

Imagine Heaven, John Burke. Baker Books, 2015.

The Reason for God, Timothy Keller. Riverhead Books, 2008.

The Christ Culture, Keith Carroll. Relate 2 God Press, 2016.

Why I Believe, D. James Kennedy. Word Publishing, 1999.

Angels, Michael S. Heiser, Lexham Press, 2018.

The Incredible Power of Prayer, Roger J. Morneau. Review and Herald Publishing Association, 1977.

Believe It, Nick Foles with Joshua Cooley. Nick Foles. Tyndale Momentum, 2018.

Save me From Myself, Brian "Head" Welch. Harper One, 2007.

A Second Chance at Heaven, Tamara Laroux. Emanate Books, 2011.

Everyday Theology, Gabriel Etzel. B&H Academic, 2017.

Introducing Christian Doctrine, Millard J. Erickson, L. Arnold Hustad. Baker Publishing Group, 2018.

Survey of the History of Christianity, Mark Nickens. Prince Press, 2018.

About the Author

JAMES WEAGLEY proudly claims the beautiful, quaint little town of Mendham, NJ as his hometown and grew up at The Seeing Eye Breeding Division property outside of town where his father served as director. He attended St. Joseph Catholic School and Mendham High School. After receiving his bachelor's and master's degrees from Lock Haven and East Stroudsburg Universities respectively, he has worked his entire career in the field of sports medicine.

He has lived his entire life in Lancaster County, Pennsylvania. His family includes wife, Karen, sons, Jeremy and Matthew, and daughter Katie. He is also a proud "Papa" to grandchildren, Elizabeth and Eomer, and a highly anticipated third grandchild on the way. Completing the family is Zoey the dog.